Best Backyard Recipes from Around the World

100 Quick and Easy Grilling Recipes

Sarah Spencer

Copyrights

All rights reserved © Sarah Spencer and The Cookbook Publisher. No part of this publication or the information in it may be quoted from or reproduced in any form by means such as printing, scanning, photocopying, or otherwise without prior written permission of the copyright holder.

Disclaimer and Terms of Use

Effort has been made to ensure that the information in this book is accurate and complete. However, the author and the publisher do not warrant the accuracy of the information, text, and graphics contained within the book due to the rapidly changing nature of science, research, known and unknown facts, and internet. The author and the publisher do not hold any responsibility for errors, omissions, or contrary interpretation of the subject matter herein. This book is presented solely for motivational and informational purposes only.

The recipes provided in this book are for informational purposes only and are not intended to provide dietary advice. A medical practitioner should be consulted before making any changes in diet. Additionally, recipe cooking times may require adjustment depending on age and quality of appliances. Readers are strongly urged to take all precautions to ensure ingredients are fully cooked in order to avoid the dangers of foodborne illnesses. The recipes and suggestions provided in this book are solely the opinion of the author. The author and publisher do not take any responsibility for any consequences that may result due to following the instructions provided in this book.

ISBN: 978-1535146159

Printed in the United States

Contents

INTRODUCTION 1
   GRILLING METHODS FROM AROUND THE WORLD 2
   MEAT SAFETY 4
   BARBECUE COOKING TIPS 5
NORTH AMERICA'S BARBECUE RECIPES 7
   KANSAS-CITY STYLE GRILLED RIBS 7
   CAROLINA PULLED PORK SANDWICH 9
   MEXICAN FISH TACOS 11
   GRILLED CHICKEN BURGERS WITH SLAW 13
   MEMPHIS-STYLE DRY RIBS 15
   CHICKEN WINGS WITH CELERY DIPPING SAUCE AND HONEY GLAZE 17
   MEXICAN TEQUILA GRILLED CHICKEN 19
   CLASSIC GRILLED VEGETABLE SKEWERS 20
   PORK TACOS WITH PINEAPPLE SALSA 21
   EAST COAST GRILLED STEAK WITH CHEESE 23
   TRADITIONAL SPICY PORK SKEWERS 24
   BARBECUED PORK WITH RED SLAW 25
   BEER CAN CHICKEN DINNER 27
   AMERICAN BURGER WITH HORSERADISH AND CHEDDAR CHEESE ... 29
   BARBECUED STEAK WITH GREEN BEANS AND CHIMICHURRI SAUCE 30
   MEXICAN PEANUT CHICKEN SKEWERS 31
   TURKEY DRUMSTICKS WITH GARLIC AND CHIPOTLES 34
   BARBECUED PORK TENDERLOIN WITH GOAT CHEESE 35
   GRILLED CHICKEN WITH MANGO SALSA 37
   HEALTHY CHICKEN PAILLARDS 38
   TRADITIONAL TEXAS-STYLE HOT DOG 39
   GRILLED RIB-EYE STEAK WITH BLUE CHEESE 41
   HOT AND SWEET BARBECUED SALMON 42
   SOUTHERN-WAY BOURBON STICKY RIBS 43
CARIBBEAN'S BARBECUE RECIPES 45
   THE CARIBBEAN GRILLED CHICKEN 45
   TRADITIONAL DRUNKEN GRILLED CHICKEN 46
   SPICY PORK CHOPS WITH POTATOES 47
   BARBECUED CHICKEN WITH CILANTRO SALSA 49
   SHRIMP SCAMPI SKEWERS WITH MANGO SALSA 51
   BACKYARD BARBECUE JERK GRILLED CHICKEN 52
   CARIBBEAN ASADO WITH CHIMICHURRI 53
   BARBECUED CORN WITH COCONUT SAUCE 54

CUBAN SPICY MOJO CHICKEN 55

SOUTH AMERICA'S BARBECUE RECIPES 57
BARBECUED PORK SKEWERS WITH MELON SALAD 57
FLATHEAD FISH FILLETS 59
GRILLED CHEESE STUFFED CHICKEN BREASTS 61
BARBECUED PORK BELLY 63
ARGENTINIAN SKEWERS WITH STEAK SAUCE 64
CHURRASCO DE PICANHA WITH BROWN BUTTER 67
ASADO BEEF RIBS WITH WINE MARINADE 64
BARBECUED CHIVITO 69
MATAMBRE BEEF WITH CHEESE 70
BARBECUED CAIPIRINHA SKEWERS 82

ASIA'S BARBECUE RECIPES 71
FARRO SALAD WITH SHERRY VINAIGRETTE 71
VIETNAMESE GRILLED PORK WITH NOODLES 73
SPICY CHICKEN KEBABS WITH PAPAYA SALAD 75
BARBECUED PRAWNS WITH GARLIC AND SOY SAUCE 77
TRADITIONAL INDIAN LAMB SKEWERS 78
SWEET ASIAN BARBECUED SALMON 79
CLASSIC CHICKEN ASIAN SKEWERS 80
TRADITIONAL KOREAN RIBS 81
SPICY CHICKEN SATAY WITH PEANUT SAUCE 82
GRILLED SALMON WITH MASALA SALSA 85
KOREAN-STYLE BARBECUED CHICKEN 87
BARBECUED SALMON WITH HONEY AND LIME 86
BARBECUED SCALLOPS AND EGGPLANT 87
TANDOORI VEGETARIAN KEBABS 90
THAI-STYLE BARBECUED BEEF SALAD 90
MISO CHICKEN SKEWERS 93
ADANA-STYLE KEBAB 95
GRILLED GALBI 96
GRILLED JOHN DORY WITH SALT KOJI 97
KOFTA-STYLE KEBABS 98
JOOJEH KEBAP WITH LEMON AND PEPPER 99
GRILLED GAI YANG 99
TRADITIONAL MALAYSIAN CHICKEN SATAY 101
KOREAN BARBECUED BRISKET 103

EUROPE'S BARBECUE RECIPES 105
BARBECUED CHICKEN WITH WHOLE GRAIN ORZO 105
BARBECUED LAMB CHOPS 107
BARBECUED CHICKEN WITH PARMESAN AND SPINACH 108

- Grilled Spanish Potatoes 109
- Barbecued Mediterranean Fish 110
- Chicken Breasts with Parsley and Mint Sauce 111
- Greek-style Barbecued Seafood 113
- Lamb Chops with Garlic Salsa 113
- Barbecued Chicken from Tuscany 116
- Spanish Shrimps with Garlic and Thyme 117
- Greek Rolled Minced Lamb with Tzatziki 118
- Cypriot Sheftalia 121
- Barbecued Chicken with Piri-Piri Sauce 119

AFRICA'S BARBECUE RECIPES 121
- Smoked Chicken Wings with Mint, Dates and Chilies 123
- Grilled Lamb Sosatie 125
- Moroccan-Style Lamb Kebabs 127
- Grilled Mechoui with Yogurt and Mint 128
- Traditional South African Braai 129
- Grilled Eggplants with Warm Grilled Bread 131
- Peanut Chicken Skewers with Yogurt 133
- Whole Brined Fish with Ujeni Ndiwo and Nsima 135
- Hanger Steak with Basting Mix and Biryani Spices 137
- Spicy Shish Kebab with Pepper 139

OCEANIA'S BARBECUE RECIPES 141
- Barbecued Swordfish 141
- Quickly Fried Squid with Garlic 142
- Filipino-style Pork Skewers 143
- Grilled Avocado with Mint and Black Pepper 144
- Australian Steak with Grilled Corn Cobs 145
- Baby Pork Ribs with Rosemary and Vincotto 146
- Pork Ribs with Orange Marinade 147
- Chicken Wings with Grilled Corn Cobs 148
- Barbecued Lobster with Tomalley Butter 149
- Grilled Lamb with Feta and Zucchini 150

CONCLUSION 151
ABOUT THE AUTHOR .... ERROR! BOOKMARK NOT DEFINED.
- More Books from Sarah Spencer 152

APPENDIX 155
- Barbecue Grilling Times and Tips 155
- Cooking Conversion Charts 160

Introduction

Barbecue cooking is the oldest cooking method that ever existed. Thousands of years ago, our ancestors roasted meat and vegetables over a live fire. Today, the situation is no different — we grill various foods and enjoy sharing a good barbecue with family and friends.

Here is a list of some reasons why barbecue cooking should take up an important part in your diet:

- **Extremely easy to cook.** You know the feeling — you're really hungry and you don't plan to waste a lot of time in preparing your meal. In these cases, you can just start your barbecue and begin grilling. Simply choose from an incredible range of great dipping sauces and marinades that are prepared simply by combining all the ingredients. Or don't even marinate it, just use salt and pepper to season the food to taste and start grilling!

- **Great for family and neighborhood gatherings.** There's no better reason to get your family together than a barbecue. Whether you are just looking to have a pleasant afternoon with your family, or you want to call the guys and chat over a couple of beers while the meat is grilling — turn up the music and the party can start!

- **Exercise makes the master.** This is totally true when it comes to grilling. If you get your own barbecue and dedicate yourself to improving this skill, you will soon be considered the best grill master in your neighborhood and wider area.

- **No need to as much oil.** The beauty of the barbecue cooking method is that it lets your food cook in its own juices. If you decide to roast a chicken, you can put a drip tray underneath to catch the juices that come out during barbecuing, and then use it for additional basting.

- **Eat with your hands.** Yes, there is nothing better than throwing away spoons and forks and eating with your bare hands. And yes, there is also the beauty of licking your fingers. How else can you totally savor the flavor?

Grilling Methods from Around the World

Different parts of the world have different cultures, and the situation is completely the same when it comes to barbecue. Meat and fire are an ideal pair, so let's take a look at how it is done in various parts of the world:

- **Southern-Style U.S.** When it comes to Southern people, it's not only about the barbecuing, it's also about smoking. They usually smoke their meat for a couple of hours, and perhaps simply finish it up on a grill with higher heat. The main thing you notice when you cook your meat slowly is that it becomes so tender it is literally falling apart by the time you eat.

- **Asado.** This is a method seen all the way across South America, especially in Argentina, Chile, and Uruguay. With asado, you usually place large slabs of meat vertically near or above the heat, allowing it to baste in its own juices. It is believed that asado comes from the old gaucho tradition, so the beef is the meat of choice for this style.

- **Braai.** Barbecue is so popular in South Africa that it even has its own national day (September 24). It is not much different than the common method of grilling the meat over the fire, except that South Africans prefer a charcoal grill. Make sure to try chicken kebabs called sosaties, as well as amazing lamb chops.

- **Jerk.** This style is used in the Caribbean region, especially Jamaica, and it is basically a seasoning blend. This complex spice blend should be massaged into your meats and poultry.

- **Shish Kebab.** This is another version of barbecue known throughout the world. Its country of origin is Turkey and it is one of the most common barbecue meals there. It is cooked over an open flame, and lamb and beef are the chosen meats to go with.

- **Satay.** This type of skewered meat is served in Malaysia, Thailand, and Indonesia, and a mandatory thing to go with the skewers are various dipping sauces.

- **Yakitori.** If you've guessed by the name, you guessed right that this is a grilled meat served in Japan. It is basically barbecued chicken meat on skewers, although it can refer to other meat types. Yakitori or kushiyaki (in cases when non-poultry items are grilled) is served in bars as snacks, where guests can ask for shio – grilled meat with salt or a version with the famous tare sauce — a mix of mirin, salty soy sauce, sake, and sugar.

- **Shrimp on the Barbie.** This is a favorite dish in Australia. Barbecue is called 'barbie' in The Land Down Under, and shrimps are their specialty. With a unique baste, you get a truly Aussie taste with your meat.

Meat Safety

Although this is not mentioned in the recipe part of our cookbook, the most important thing you need to consider is that it is cooked right. This is why you need to be sure when determining whether your meat is cooked 'just right'. The best way to measure this and get an accurate result is to use a thermometer that will give you an instant read of the meat's internal temperature. Avoid determining doneness of the meat by using your own judgment. Use the thermometer and have a precise measurement, as this is a totally sure way of avoiding potential bacteria found in the meat.

Below find a table with the safe minimums of internal meat temperature in Fahrenheit degrees as suggested by the USDA for different types of meat:

Meat	USDA Safe Minimum
Chicken & Turkey	
Whole	165°F
Parts	165°F
Stuffed	165°F
Ground	165°F
Beef, Veal, & Lamb	
Rare	125°F + 3 minutes rest
Medium Rare	130 – 135 °F
Medium	135 – 140°F
Medium Well	145°F + 3 minutes rest
Well done	155°F + 3 minutes rest
Ground	160°F
Pork	
Medium rare	145°F + 3 minute rest
Medium	150°F
Well done	160°F
Ground	160°F

You will find a more detailed table in the appendix at the end of the book.

Barbecue Cooking Tips

Here are some tips you can use to prepare better food when you cook with your barbecue.

- **What type of barbecue to pick.** The question of whether a charcoal or a gas grill should be used has been a topic of debate for various barbecue experts from around the world. There is no evidence as to which one is healthier, but on one hand, gas burns cleaner, and on the other hand, the charcoal grill can give you significantly tastier food.

- **Preheat your grill.** If you preheat your barbecue before putting the meat on it, you will prevent sticking, kill any bacteria on contact and allow the meat to stay moist. You should preheat your grill to 250-300°F if you are going for low heat, 300-350°F for medium, 350-400°F for medium high, and up to 450°F for high heat.

- **Oil the grates.** As it is mentioned in some of the recipes, make sure to oil the grates using a paper towel soaked with vegetable oil. Rub the paper towel on the rack while holding it with tongs.

- **Safety first.** Food safety must be your top priority. Use a thermometer for measuring the internal temperature of the meat, and make sure to have a different cutting board, plates and utensils for raw and cooked foods.

- **Let it rest.** When you finish with grilling your meat, transfer it to a clean platter, cover with foil, and give it about 10 minutes to rest. This will enable the juices within the meat to be distributed equally.

- **Be organized.** Make sure you have enough surface that you be able to work. Gather all equipment and other things you will need during the process, such as ways of keeping any raw meat away from the cooked. Also, make sure to stay by your grill the whole time you are barbecuing, for safety and best results.

- **Clean your barbecue.** Make sure that you clean your barbecue before you start cooking and after you finish with barbecuing. Don't be lazy; keep your grill in shape to prolong its lifespan.

North America's Barbecue Recipes

Kansas-City Style Grilled Ribs

Kansas City is famous for its barbecue, and one of the most delicious recipes is this one for ribs we are offering. You cannot miss with choosing this recipe for your traditional American barbecue.

Serves 10-20

Ingredients:
10 pork baby back rib racks
American mustard

For the rub:
⅓ cup salt
⅓ cup paprika
½ cup brown sugar
¼ cup white sugar
1 tablespoon celery salt
1 tablespoon seasoned salt
1 tablespoon ground black pepper
2 teaspoons smoked paprika
1 teaspoon onion powder
1 teaspoon garlic powder

For basting:
1 cup apple juice
2 tablespoons brown sugar

Directions:
1. Trim and arrange the ribs by cutting the cartilage at the base of the bones to form a shape similar to a rectangle. Cut any fat left on the meaty part, and pull off the silvery membrane.

2. Combine the ingredients for the rub and whisk them together. Use the American mustard to lightly coat the ribs and then sprinkle with the rub.
3. Use your smoker to cook the ribs at 230°F, making sure to place the meaty side up. You should cook until all the spices have set, which should not take more than 3 hours total. You can check if the spices have set by simply using your nail to perform a scratch test.
4. Mix the apple juice and brown sugar until sugar is dissolved completely and put mixture into a spray bottle. Take the meat off the smoker and spray with apple juice mixture on both sides. Use foil to wrap the ribs tightly and put them back on the smoker once they are covered.
5. Smoke for an additional hour, using a toothpick to see how tender the ribs are. Put a toothpick between the bones and once you are satisfied with tenderness, remove them from the smoker and remove the foil.
6. Place the ribs back on the smoker, unwrapped, for an additional hour. Occasionally glaze them with the apple juice mixture.

Carolina Pulled Pork Sandwich

Once you try pulled pork, you will be absolutely charmed. This recipe is used primarily in the Carolinas in the United States and enjoys a great reputation.

Serves 18 and more

Ingredients:
1 pork scotch fillet, around 9 pounds
1 cup apple juice
Hamburger buns
Coleslaw
Barbecue sauce

For pulled pork marinade:
2 tablespoons salt
2 tablespoons white sugar
2 tablespoons paprika
2 tablespoons dry mustard powder
1 tablespoon ground black pepper
1 tablespoon cayenne pepper

For red dip:
1 cup cider vinegar
1 cup ketchup
½ cup white vinegar
⅓ cup brown vinegar
1 tablespoon brown sugar
3 teaspoons salt
½ teaspoon hot sauce
½ teaspoon ground black pepper
¼ teaspoon cayenne pepper

Directions:
1. Prepare the marinade by combining all the ingredients together and sprinkling it over the pork.
2. Make a red dip by combining all the ingredients for it and boiling them together. Let it cool down to room temperature.

3. Set your smoker to 260°F. Cook the pork for approximately 4 hours. Perform a scratch test to see if the marinade has set.
4. Combine half of the red dip with 1 cup of apple juice.
5. Once the marinade has set, sprinkle with apple juice and red dip mixture. Repeat this every half hour for the next 3 hours.
6. Use foil to wrap the meat, and try to save the juices.
7. As you pull the meat apart, remove any fat and try to keep the pieces as big as possible. When you finish with pulling the meat, massage the other half of the red dip into the meat.
8. The final step is to add the juices you kept.
9. Assemble the sandwich placing a generous portion of pork on each bun, top with coleslaw and bun. Serve it with your favorite barbecue sauce on the side.

Mexican Fish Tacos

This authentic Mexican recipe will provide you with a delicious marinated and spicy barbecued fish. To do it exactly as they do it in Mexico, serve with warm corn tortillas.

Serves 8-12

Ingredients:
Marinade
2 tablespoons vegetable oil
1 onion, roughly chopped
2 garlic cloves, chopped
1 tablespoon achiote paste
1 tomato, cut into wedges
Juice of ½ an orange
Juice of ½ a lime
2 Guajillo chilies, soaked for 20 minutes in hot water, drained
¾ cup beer

Salsa
2 roma (plum) tomatoes
3 habanero chilies
1 onion, peeled and quartered
Handful of cilantro (cilantro) leaves

Fish
1 whole snapper, or another firm white-fleshed fish, gutted but not scaled, about 3-5 pounds
1 teaspoon garlic oil

To serve
Fresh corn tortillas

Directions:
1. Prepare the marinade by heating vegetable oil in a pan to a medium temperature. Put in the onion and garlic, cook until they soften, and then add the achiote paste and tomato wedges. Combine nicely before adding the orange and lime

juice, softened chilies, and beer. Make sure to stir well so the achiote can dissolve.
2. Use a blender to process the mixture, and then cook it for additional half hour. Let it cool down.
3. Prepare the salsa by putting the tomatoes, chilies and onion on your barbecue. Grill for approximately 10 minutes, flipping to ensure that both sides are grilled. Transfer all ingredients to a mortar and pound it with the pestle until it becomes a chunky mixture. Add the cilantro leaves and stir.
4. Use a knife and split the fish along the backbone. Rub garlic oil on the inside part of the fish and season it with pepper according to your taste. Sprinkle the fish with marinade on the flesh side, and put it in a wire basket.
5. Grill it for approximately 8 minutes, flipping and basting regularly. Begin with the skin side down.
6. Take the fish off the grill and flake it, discarding the bones. Serve with corn tortillas and salsa.

Grilled Chicken Burgers with Slaw

Burgers can also be made with chicken meat, and this recipe shows just how delicious these burgers can be when prepared with the right sauces.

Serves 4

Ingredients:
1 tablespoon butter
1 small red onion, one half sliced in rings and one half diced
2 cloves garlic, chopped
2 tablespoons tomato paste
1 teaspoon sugar
1 tablespoon Worcestershire sauce
1 tablespoon hot sauce
1 ¼ pounds ground chicken
1 tablespoon grill seasoning
3 tablespoons extra virgin olive oil
2 tablespoons honey
1 lemon juice
3 tablespoons sweet pickle relish
2 cups shredded cabbage combination
Salt and pepper
4 sKaiser rolls

Directions:
1. Use a small skillet to melt the butter over medium heat. Put in the chopped onions, garlic, and tomato paste, and simmer for about 5 minutes. Add the sugar gradually and transfer it to a bowl to cool down for 5 minutes. Add the Worcestershire and hot sauce, and mix well.
2. Put the chicken into the bowl and combine, making sure to evenly distribute all the flavors. Form 4 patties and wash up.
3. Preheat your grill to medium-high heat. Grill the burgers for approximately 5 minutes on each side.
4. Mix the olive oil, honey, and lemon juice in a dish. Add the relish, sliced onions, and cabbage mix. Season with salt and pepper and mix to coat.

5. When serving, top the bun bottoms with slaw, put burgers on, and then put the bun tops over the burgers.

Memphis-Style Dry Ribs

Memphis is famous for its wet and dry ribs, and we are offering you a traditional recipe for dry pork loin ribs.

Serves 4-6

Ingredients:
2 slabs pork baby back ribs, about 2 ¼ pounds each

Rub:
¾ cup sugar in the raw
½ cup salt
¼ cup paprika
2 tablespoons finely ground black pepper
1 tablespoon granulated garlic
1 tablespoon onion powder
1 tablespoon ground cumin
1 tablespoon chili powder
1 teaspoon dry mustard
1 teaspoon ground cilantro
½ teaspoon cayenne pepper
½ teaspoon ground allspice

Directions:
1. Prepare the rub by mixing all the ingredients, combining them well. Keep the marinade in an airtight container.
2. Peel the membrane off the ribs and remove any excess fat. Coat them nicely with the marinade and refrigerate for at least 30 minutes and up to 4 hours.
3. Preheat the barbecue to medium heat.
4. Take the ribs out of the marinade and place them on the barbecue with the meaty side up. Cook both sides until done and move the pieces to a platter.
5. Lay out two large sheets of tinfoil. Move the ribs to them and fold them into a packet. Don't puncture the foil. Return the packets to the grill over medium-low heat to achieve the desired tenderness, about 1 to 1 ½ hours.

6. Move them back to the platter, discard the foil, and place the meat back on the barbecue. Drizzle with additional marinade and grill for approximately 4 minutes. Flip and repeat the process.

Chicken Wings with Celery Dipping sauce and Honey Glaze

Many Americans will say that chicken wings are their favorite kind of meat. This recipe offers an incredibly tasteful dipping sauce and gives chicken wings a great flavor.

Serves- 4-6

Ingredients:
For the wings
1 cup hot sauce
½ cup honey
6 tablespoons unsalted butter
1 tablespoon red wine vinegar
Salt
Freshly ground black pepper
24 chicken wings

For the blue cheese-celery dipping sauce
½ cup mayonnaise
½ cup Greek yogurt
1 teaspoon Worcestershire sauce
7 tablespoons finely diced celery
3 ½ tablespoons crumbled blue cheese
2 tablespoons finely chopped fresh chives
Salt
Freshly ground black pepper

Directions:
1. Preheat your grill to a medium-high temperature.
2. Make the dipping sauce by mixing all ingredients in a dish and seasoning with salt and pepper. Let it rest in the refrigerator for at least half an hour.
3. Place the hot sauce, honey, and butter in a pan and cook for approximately 5 minutes, until the butter is melted and the mixture combined. Add the vinegar and use salt and pepper to season it to your liking. Transfer half the mixture into a dish.

4. Sprinkle the chicken wings with salt and pepper, then rub the meat with the half of the sauce you transferred to a dish. Place the wings on the grill and barbecue each side for approximately five minutes.
5. Take it off the grill and toss with the other half of the sauce. Serve with the dipping sauce.

Mexican Tequila Grilled Chicken

When you think of tequila, you think of Mexico. We are grateful to the people of this country for creating this recipe, which gives chicken a whole different taste.

Serves 6

Ingredients:
½ cup gold tequila
1 cup freshly squeezed lime juice
½ cup freshly squeezed orange juice
1 tablespoon chili powder
1 tablespoon minced fresh jalapeno pepper
1 tablespoon minced fresh garlic
2 teaspoons salt
1 teaspoon freshly ground black pepper
3 whole (or 6 split) boneless chicken breasts, skin on

Directions:
1. Mix the tequila, lime juice, orange juice, chili powder, jalapeno pepper, garlic, salt, and black pepper in a big bowl. When combined nicely, put in the chicken breasts and flip to coat. Cover the bowl and refrigerate overnight.
2. Rub the grates of your barbecue with oil and preheat it to medium-high heat.
3. Take the chicken out of the marinade. Season with salt and pepper to your liking.
4. Grill the chicken skin side down for approximately 5 minutes, then flip it and grill for additional 10 minutes. Transfer to a serving platter, cover it, and let it cool down for about 5 minutes.

Classic Grilled Vegetable Skewers

This is a great recipe for a family barbecue, as your kids can participate equally in preparing these tasteful skewers.

Serves: 8 sides

Ingredients:
2 red peppers
2 red onions
8 rosemary sprigs
1 tablespoon olive oil
½ teaspoon salt
½ teaspoon cracked pepper

Directions:
1. Prepare your grill by preheating it to medium-high heat.
2. Use a knife to slice the peppers and onions into cubes of approximately 2 inches. Thread it onto the rosemary springs.
3. Sprinkle with olive oil, season with salt and pepper, and place them on a grill. Grill until they become tender, no longer than 15 minutes.

Pork Tacos with Pineapple Salsa

Another Mexican recipe, this time an important part of this country's street food. You will be so thrilled you will lick your fingers.

Serves 6-8

Ingredients:
2 pounds pork tenderloin

For the pork marinade:
1 cup chipotle in adobo (tinned)
6 cloves garlic
4 tablespoons achiote paste
¼ cup apple cider vinegar
2 tablespoons honey
1 bunch chopped fresh cilantro
2 tablespoons olive oil
2 teaspoons salt
2 teaspoons ground black pepper

For the pineapple salsa:
1 ripe pineapple, well skinned, sliced thin, diced
1 red pepper, diced
1 finely diced bird's eye chili
1 bunch finely chopped cilantro
½ cup fresh lime juice
¼ cup orange juice
2 tablespoons brown sugar
2 tablespoons chipotle powder
1 pinch salt
Tortillas and fresh Mexican cheese, for serving

Directions:
1. In a large bowl, mix all the ingredients for the marinade. Add the pork and turn to coat. Cover with plastic wrap, and put it into the refrigerator overnight.
2. Preheat your barbecue to medium-high. Slice the pork into thin strips, and grill for approximately 1 minute on each side.

3. Prepare the pineapple salsa by mixing the pineapple, pepper, chili, and cilantro in a bowl. Add all the remaining ingredients and whisk well.
4. Serve the pork with warm tortillas, fresh cheese, and pineapple salsa.

East Coast Grilled Steak with Cheese

Amazing American steak sandwich with cheese, just the way they prepare it in Philadelphia.

Serves 2-4

Ingredients:
2 tablespoons unsalted butter
2 tablespoons all-purpose flour
2 cups whole milk
6-7 ounces of grated cheddar
2 teaspoons dry mustard
Salt and freshly ground pepper
2 beef tenderloin steaks, 14 ounces each
2 tablespoons olive oil
4 Italian rolls, split in half and grilled

For the topping
Grilled mushrooms, cut
Grilled green peppers, cut
Grilled yellow and red onions, chopped
Grilled Cubano peppers, cut

Directions:
1. Preheat your barbecue to high.
2. In a saucepan, melt the butter over medium heat. Add the flour and cook for approximately 1 minute. Whisking constantly, slowly pour in the milk and continue cooking until thickened. Add the cheese and continue cooking until melted. Stir in the dry mustard and season with salt and pepper.
3. Rub the fillets with oil and season with salt and pepper.
4. Grill for approximately 3 minutes per side. Let them cool down for about 5 minutes. Cut the meat into ¼-inch slices.
5. Cut ¾ of the way into the rolls, and fill each with a couple of beef slices, cheese sauce, and the toppings of your choice. Once the sandwiches are assembled, grill them briefly to heat through.

Traditional Spicy Pork Skewers

If you are into spicy food, this American pork recipe will give you fireworks of great flavor, exactly the way you like it.

Serves: 4

Ingredients:
¼ cup low-sodium soy sauce
¼ cup oyster sauce
3 tablespoons finely chopped cilantro leaves and stems
2 tablespoons finely chopped garlic
2 tablespoons sugar
1 teaspoon freshly ground black pepper
24-ounce pork fillet, cut into 16 pieces
16 wooden skewers, soaked in cold water for 30 minutes

For the chili sauce
½ cup fresh lime juice
¼ cup fish sauce
1 tablespoon soy sauce
2 teaspoons sugar
1 fresh Thai red chili, finely diced
1 shallot, finely diced

Directions:
1. In a medium bowl, mix together the soy sauce, oyster sauce, cilantro, garlic, sugar, and black pepper.
2. Thread the pork on the skewers and then coat it nicely with the marinade. Cover with plastic wrap and put it into the refrigerator for 1-4 hours.
3. In a separate bowl, mix the ingredients for the chili sauce. Once mixed, cover it with plastic wrap and let it rest at room temperature for one hour.
4. Preheat your barbecue to medium-high. Take the skewers out of the marinade and grill them on both sides for approximately 5 minutes.
5. Warm the chili sauce, and serve it with the pork.

Barbecued Pork with Red Slaw

If you are looking for fine barbecued pork with a healthy touch of red slaw, look no more and try this amazing recipe.

Serves: 4-6

Ingredients:
For the pork
¼ cup fresh cilantro leaves, finely chopped
1 tablespoon fresh lime juice
1 tablespoon vegetable oil
1 teaspoon chipotle chili powder
2 cloves garlic, minced
¼ small red onion, very thinly sliced
1 pork fillet, about 2 pounds, cut into ½-inch thick slices on an angle
Salt and freshly ground black pepper

For the red slaw
2 cups shredded red cabbage
¼ cup fresh cilantro leaves, finely chopped
1 tablespoon vegetable oil
1 tablespoon cider vinegar
¼ teaspoon chipotle chili powder
1 small red pepper, very thinly sliced
¼ small red onion, very thinly sliced
Salt and freshly ground black pepper
8 corn tortillas
8 teaspoons reduced-fat sour cream
Lime wedges, for serving

Directions:
1. Mix the cilantro, lime juice, oil, chili powder, garlic, and onions in a big bowl. Put in the pork and coat it nicely.
2. In a large bowl, mix the cabbage, cilantro, oil, vinegar, chili powder, red pepper, red onions, and just a touch of salt and pepper (about ¼ teaspoon of each). Whisk it nicely.

3. Take the pork from the marinade and sprinkle it with just a touch of salt and pepper (again, ¼ teaspoon of each). Grill for approximately 5 minutes on each side and move to a big serving platter.
4. Grill the tortillas for approximately 1 minute and move them to individual serving plates. Divide the pork and slaw evenly among the tortillas, and then top each with sour cream. Serve lime wedges on the side.

Beer Can Chicken Dinner

This is an easy, but ideal, American chicken recipe, especially if you are planning an afternoon party with your friends.

Serves 4-6

Ingredients:
1 whole chicken, about 3-4 pounds
6 cloves garlic, peeled and minced
1 tablespoon dry rosemary
Olive oil to coat
Salt and pepper to taste
1 beer in a tall can
2 tablespoons brown sugar

<u>Vegetables:</u>
1 zucchini cubed,
2 carrots, cubed,
1 celery rib, cubed
1 onion, cubed
2 red potatoes, cubed,
1 green or red bell pepper, diced
2 tablespoons olive oil
1 teaspoon garlic powder
1 teaspoon thyme

Directions:
1. Stuff the chicken cavity with a mixture of garlic, rosemary, salt and olive oil.
2. Oil the grates with cooking spray and heat to medium, about 350°F.
3. Empty a beer can and reserve beer for basting. Place the whole chicken on the empty beer can, making sure that cavity-side is down and goes over the can.
4. Mixed the chopped vegetables in a large aluminum tray. Add the olive oil, garlic powder and thyme. Stir a few times to coat well. Drizzle with 1 cup of the reserved beer.

Make a large enough space in the middle to place the beer can chicken. Place in the middle of the grate. The cooking juices of the chicken will add flavor to the vegetables.
5. Place reminder in a spray bottle with 2 tablespoons brown sugar. Mix well. Spray every 10-15 minutes.
6. Grill with barbecue cover down for about an hour to an hour and a half, or until the meat is cooked through and juices run clear when poked with a fork. Let rest 10 minutes before carving.

American Burger with Horseradish and Cheddar Cheese

Classic American hamburger recipe ideal for family picnics, as it is very easy to prepare.

Serves 8

Ingredients:
2 pounds freshly minced beef brisket
16 slices Cheddar cheese, cut into thinner than ¼-inch slices
8 leaves romaine lettuce
Gherkin pickles, chopped
Freshly ground salt and black pepper
Ketchup
8 buns

Grilled onions
2 big onions, cut crossways into thinner than ¼-inch slices
Freshly ground salt and black pepper
2 tablespoons olive oil

Horseradish mustard
8 tablespoons Dijon mustard
2 tablespoons drained horseradish

Directions:
1. Mix the horseradish and mustard in a bowl and combine well.
2. Brush the onions with olive oil and season them with salt and pepper. Grill for approximately 4 minutes per side.
3. Split the beef into 8 burgers and sprinkle salt and pepper to your liking. Grill them for approximately 4 minutes per side.
4. In the last minute of grilling, add 2 slices of cheese to every burger and let the cheese melt.
5. Split each bun and place a burger in the middle. Top the burgers with horseradish mustard, grilled onions, lettuce, ketchup and gherkins before placing the other half of the bun on top.

Barbecued Steak with Green Beans and Chimichurri Sauce

This is a healthy American recipe for a grilled steak. Fans of green beans will certainly enjoy these steaks.

Serves 4

Ingredients:
¾ pound green beans, trimmed
1 pint grape tomatoes, halved
1 tablespoon olive oil, plus more for grill grates
Salt and freshly ground pepper
4 New York strip steaks, about 1-inch thick trimmed of excess fat

For the chimichurri sauce
½ small clove of garlic
¼ cup fresh herbs, such as parsley, mint, and cilantro
1 tablespoon red wine vinegar
1 tablespoon extra-virgin olive oil
1 tablespoon water
Salt and freshly ground black pepper

Directions:
1. Put a double-layered piece of foil on a tray and fold the edges up to form a rim. Put in the green beans and tomatoes, add 1 tablespoon of olive oil, and sprinkle with salt and pepper to your liking.
2. Prepare the chimichurri sauce by mixing the garlic, herbs, vinegar, olive oil, and water in a blender. Blend them nicely and then season with salt and pepper.
3. Sprinkle the steak with salt and pepper to your taste.
4. Prepare your grill by oiling the grates. Place the foil tray on the grill, turning it occasionally to cook the beans. You will need approximately 15 minutes.
5. Place the steaks on the barbecue and grill each side for approximately 5 minutes. Transfer them to a cutting board and let them rest for about 5 minutes before cutting them.

Mexican Peanut Chicken Skewers

It might seem like a bit of a venture to prepare this delicious Mexican recipe, but it will be worth every minute once you taste these incredible chicken skewers with peanut sauce.

Serves: 2-4

Ingredients:
2-3 boneless skinless chicken breasts, pounded to ½ inch thickness and into strips
24 wooden skewers, soaked in water for 30 minutes
½ cup fresh squeezed orange juice
¼ cup fresh squeezed lime juice
2 tablespoons honey
2 tablespoons canola oil
2 tablespoons ancho chili powder
3 cloves garlic, coarsely chopped
Salt and freshly ground black pepper
Butter lettuce leaves, to serve
Fresh mint leaves, for garnish
Chopped roasted peanuts, for garnish

For the mesa BARBECUE sauce
2 tablespoons oil
1 large Spanish onion, coarsely chopped
5 cloves garlic, coarsely chopped
2 ½ cups tinned plum tomatoes and juices, pureed
1 cup water
4 tablespoons ketchup
4 tablespoons red wine vinegar
4 tablespoons Worcestershire sauce
3 tablespoons Dijon mustard
3 tablespoons dark brown sugar
2 tablespoons honey
¼ cup molasses
3 tablespoons ancho chili powder
3 tablespoons pasilla chili powder
2-4 canned chipotle chilies in adobo, pureed (depending on how spicy you like it)

Salt and freshly ground black pepper

For the peanut barbecue sauce
1 tablespoon oil
1 3-inch piece fresh ginger, peeled and finely chopped
1 cup mesa barbecue sauce, (below) or store-bought barbecue sauce
2 cups homemade chicken stock or low-sodium canned chicken broth
2 tablespoons soy sauce
4 tablespoons peanut butter
2 tablespoons chipotle in adobo puree
2 tablespoons honey
Salt and freshly ground black pepper

For the red cabbage slaw
½ head red cabbage, finely shredded
1 small red onion, halved and thinly sliced
4 tablespoons rice wine vinegar
½ cup freshly squeezed orange juice
4 tablespoons olive oil
1 tablespoon honey
6 tablespoons chopped cilantro leaves
Salt and freshly ground black pepper

Directions:
1. To prepare the mesa barbecue sauce, heat the 2 tablespoons of oil in a pan over medium heat. Put in the onion and cook for approximately 4 minutes. Add the garlic and cook for an additional minute. Add the tomatoes and water, bring it to a boil and then simmer for approximately 10 minutes. Put in the remaining ingredients and simmer for another 30 minutes, making sure to stir occasionally. Move the sauce to a blender and process until it becomes smooth. Sprinkle with salt and pepper to your liking. Pour it into a bowl and let it cool down at room temperature.
2. To make the peanut barbecue sauce, heat the oil in a pan over medium heat. Put in the ginger and add sauté it until softened. Add the barbecue sauce and chicken stock and continue cooking over medium-high.

Stir from time to time and when it is reduced to half, add the soy sauce, peanut butter, chipotle puree, and honey. Cook until it gets thick, about 20-30 minutes. Taste, and season with salt and pepper as required.
3. For the slaw, mix the cabbage and onion in a big bowl. Combine the vinegar, orange juice, oil, and honey, and pour the mixture over the cabbage and onion mixture. Stir in the cilantro leaves and sprinkle with salt and pepper. Let it set for about 20 minutes.
4. Tread the chicken strips on the skewers.
5. Mix the orange juice, lime juice, honey, oil, chili powder, and garlic. Coat the chicken nicely with this marinade and refrigerate it for at least one hour and no more than 4 hours.
6. Preheat the barbecue to medium.
7. Take the chicken out of the marinade and sprinkle with salt and pepper. Place it on the barbecue and grill each side for approximately 4 minutes.
8. Take the chicken off the skewers and arrange it among the butter lettuce leaves. Sprinkle with peanut-red chili sauce and sprinkle the mint, slaw, and chopped peanuts over it.

Turkey Drumsticks with Garlic and Chipotles

Turkey is usually not a primary choice for a barbecue party in America, but this recipe deserves its place among the best ones.

Serves: 8

Ingredients:
1 cup hot water
1 cup molasses
1 cup salt
1 tablespoon black peppercorns
2 lemons, sliced
2 onions, quartered
1 head garlic, peeled with the cloves crushed
1 big bunch fresh rosemary
8 turkey drumsticks
8 cups cold water
Salt and freshly ground black pepper
¼ cup butter
Pureed canned chipotles in adobo sauce

Directions:
1. Put 1 cup of hot water into a large, non-reactive bowl. Add the molasses and salt, and stir well. Add the peppercorns, lemons, onions, garlic, and rosemary. Put the drumsticks into the marinade and add 8 cups of cold water. Put it in the refrigerator for 6 hours, ideally overnight.
2. When you are ready to cook, take the turkey out of the marinade and season it to your taste with salt and pepper.
3. Prepare your grill for indirect cooking. Place the drumsticks on the side of the barbecue opposite the charcoal. Melt the butter and drizzle it over the turkey, and close the lid. Cook until cooked through, making sure to flip and baste the drumsticks occasionally (every half hour).
4. Take the meat off the grill and brush with pureed chipotles before serving.

Barbecued Pork Tenderloin with Goat Cheese

This unusual, healthy American recipe uses goat cheese, which will give it a special flavor you will surely enjoy.

Serves: 4

Ingredients:
¼ cup Greek yogurt
4 ounces goat cheese, at room temperature (about ½ cup)
⅓ cup water
½ cup extra-virgin olive oil, divided
2 spring onions, thinly sliced
¼ cup fresh flat-leaf parsley leaves, roughly chopped
Salt and freshly ground black pepper
1 pork tenderloin, about 1 ½ pounds
2 large ripe plums, halved and pitted
5 ounces baby rocket salad mix
½ lemon, juiced

Directions:
1. Mix the yogurt with the goat cheese and ⅓ cup of water, until it becomes smooth. Add 3 tablespoons of oil, spring onions, and parsley. Sprinkle with salt and pepper.
2. Preheat the barbecue to high heat. Drizzle the pork with 1 tablespoon of oil and season it with salt and pepper. Grill each side for about 6 minutes until it becomes nicely charred.
3. Use another tablespoon of oil to brush the cut side of the plums. Season them with salt and pepper and place them on the grill, cut side down. Grill for approximately 3 minutes and move them to a serving platter.
4. Let the pork rest for about 10 minutes once it is grilled. Cut it into thin diagonal slices against the grain. Sprinkle lightly with salt.
5. Use the remaining oil and mix it with the baby rocket salad mix and lemon juice.

6. Divide the salad onto 4 serving platters, making sure that the salad takes one-half of the plate. Spoon some goat cheese sauce onto the other half, and place pork slices on top of the sauce. Add one plum half to each plate and spoon more sauce over, if you like.

Grilled Chicken with Mango Salsa

A beautiful mango sauce is what makes this recipe special and gives the chicken that exquisite flavor the whole family will enjoy

Serves: 6

Ingredients:
1 large ripe mango, peeled, pitted and roughly chopped
4 ½ tablespoons cilantro leaves, chopped
2 chipotle peppers in adobo, plus 1 tablespoon adobo sauce
2 tablespoons unseasoned rice wine vinegar
4 cloves garlic, peeled
2 tablespoons fresh lemon juice
1 tablespoon grapeseed oil, plus extra for the grill
2 teaspoons salt
1 teaspoon freshly cracked black pepper
2 pounds chicken thighs and drumsticks, bone-in, skin on

Directions:
1. Mix the mango, cilantro, chipotle peppers, vinegar, garlic, lemon juice, 1 tablespoon of oil, and salt in a blender. Process until it becomes smooth.
2. Mix the chicken with half of the mixture and place it in a plastic bag that can be resealed. Coat the chicken well and put it in the refrigerator overnight or for at least for 6 hours.
3. Place the other half of the mango mixture in a pan and simmer on low heat, for approximately 15 minutes, or until it thickens. Divide it into two portions, one for basting, and one for dipping.
4. Preheat your barbecue and coat the grates with oil. Take the chicken out of the marinade and place it on the grill.
5. Grill for approximately 20 minutes, flipping it and coating with one portion of the mango sauce every five minutes. Move to a serving dish and garnish with the last of the mango sauce.

Healthy Chicken Paillards

A paillard is a piece of meat pounded thin and cooked on a grill. Try this healthy way of preparing chicken paillards with a salad that presents a mixture of tomatoes and herbs.

Serves: 2-4

Ingredients:
2 ripe medium tomatoes (1 red and 1 yellow), cored and roughly chopped (about 1 ½ cups)
1 clove garlic, peeled and smashed
1 spring onion (white and green parts), thinly sliced
3 tablespoons extra-virgin olive oil, plus additional for brushing
2 teaspoons red wine vinegar
2 teaspoons salt, plus additional for seasoning
Freshly ground black pepper
⅓ cup torn fresh basil
3 tablespoons fresh tarragon, roughly chopped
3 tablespoons fresh flat-leaf parsley, roughly chopped
2 chicken breasts, about 8 ounces each

Directions:
1. Lay out the chicken breasts with the smooth side down. Cut a small slit down the center of the breast, allowing the knife to pierce only halfway through the meat. From the bottom of your slit, turn the knife and cut sideways toward the edge of the meat. Do not cut through the side. Do the same on the other side, and open the sliced portions outwards. Place the meat in a bag and pound it to an even thickness.
2. Mix the tomatoes, garlic, spring onion, 3 tablespoons of olive oil, vinegar, salt, and black pepper in a bowl.
3. Brush the chicken with olive oil and season with salt and black pepper liberally. Grill it for approximately 2 minutes on each side.
4. Mix the herbs with the tomatoes.
5. Divide the chicken onto 4 plates. Spoon the herb-tomato salad over or beside it and serve.

Traditional Texas-Style Hot Dog

Try this traditional recipe for hot dogs and make your afternoon barbecue truly American.

Serves: 8

Ingredients:
For the hot dogs
8 good quality beef hot dogs
8 good quality hot dog buns, split ¾ through

For the barbecue sauce
2 tablespoons rapeseed oil
1 large onion, coarsely chopped
5 cloves garlic, coarsely chopped
21 ounces canned plum tomatoes and juices, pureed
1 cup water
4 tablespoons tomato ketchup
¼ cup red wine vinegar
¼ cup Worcestershire sauce
3 tablespoons Dijon mustard
3 tablespoons dark brown sugar
2 tablespoons honey
5 tablespoons molasses
3 tablespoons ancho chili powder
3 tablespoons pasilla chili powder
2 to 4 tinned chipotle chilies in adobo, pureed
2 tablespoons sugar
Salt
Freshly ground black pepper

For the coleslaw
¾ cup mayonnaise
¼ cup white sugar
½ small white onion, grated
2 teaspoons celery seeds
3 tablespoons apple cider vinegar
Salt
Freshly ground black pepper

1 head cabbage, cored, finely shredded
1 large carrot, finely grated
Sour gherkins (not half sour), for serving

Directions:
1. To prepare the barbecue sauce, heat the oil in a pan over medium heat. Put in the onions and cook for approximately 3 minutes. Add the garlic and cook for an additional minute. Add the tomatoes and water, and bring it to a boil. Simmer for about 10 minutes. Add all the ingredients remaining for the barbecue sauce, and let it simmer for about 30 minutes, until the mixture gets thick. Stir from time to time.
2. For the slaw, mix the mayonnaise, sugar, onion, celery seeds, vinegar, salt, and pepper in a bowl. Mix in the cabbage and carrot. Let it rest for about 15 minutes.
3. Preheat your barbecue to medium. Grill the hot dogs for approximately 7 minutes, turning them occasionally. Once they are nicely browned, move them to a platter.
4. Split the buns in half and place them on the grill with the cut side down. Heat them just a bit. Brush the hot dogs with barbecue sauce, put them in the buns, and put gherkins and coleslaw over them.

Grilled Rib-Eye Steak with Blue Cheese

This incredible American steak recipe will knock you off your feet. Give it a shot and you definitely won't regret it.

Serves 4

Ingredients:
4 rib eye steaks (about 6 ounces each)
Salt and freshly ground black pepper
1 stick softened butter
1 large yellow onion, sliced
1 cup double cream
3-4 tablespoons Worcestershire sauce
¾ cup crumbled blue cheese

Directions:
1. Prepare your barbecue by heating it to medium.
2. Season the steaks with salt and pepper, and rub butter on both sides of each steak. Use only half the butter.
3. Grill the steaks for approximately 6 minutes, flipping them to make sure each side is grilled.
4. Melt the other half of the butter in a pan, and add the onions. Sauté them for approximately 8 minutes, then add the cream and Worcestershire sauce. Put in blue cheese and mix, and season with salt and pepper.
5. Pour the sauce over the steaks and serve.

Hot and Sweet Barbecued Salmon

This American recipe for barbecued salmon is very easy to prepare and is guaranteed to be a big hit.

Serves: 4

Ingredients:
2 tablespoons hot sauce, such as Frank's®
1 tablespoon packed dark brown sugar
1 teaspoon smoked paprika
¼ teaspoon cayenne pepper
2 tablespoons light mayonnaise
1 tablespoon snipped chives
8 stalks celery, very thinly sliced in half moons on an angle
½ small red onion, very thinly sliced
4 5-ounce center cut skin-on salmon fillets, about 1 inch thick
Salt and freshly ground black pepper
Vegetable oil, for oiling the grill

Directions:
1. Combine the hot sauce, brown sugar, paprika, and cayenne in one bowl.
2. Move 1 tablespoon of the mixture to a big bowl. Add the mayonnaise and whisk it together. Put in the chives, celery, and onions and combine well.
3. Season the salmon with salt and pepper to your liking. Brush the grates with oil and place the salmon on the barbecue, skin side up. Grill for about 4 minutes. Flip it and brush with some of the sauce from the first step. Continue with grilling, brushing occasionally with sauce, until the salmon is done. Serve with celery slaw.

Southern-way Bourbon Sticky Ribs

Bourbon and barbecue are a traditional couple in the southern part of the United States. Your ribs will get that particular sweetness with this bourbon sauce.

Serves: 4

Ingredients:
2 racks St-Louis-style pork ribs
Hot water to cover
2 teaspoons salt
Hot sauce and coleslaw, to serve

Bourbon barbecue sauce
1 tablespoon vegetable oil
1 onion, chopped
1 large garlic clove, chopped
⅓ cup apple cider vinegar
6 ½ tablespoons brown sugar
1 tablespoon molasses
1 cup tomato sauce
1 teaspoon Worcestershire sauce
½ cup bourbon
1 teaspoon mustard powder
1 teaspoon dried chili flakes
1 teaspoon smoked paprika
½ cup water

Collard greens
½ cups unsalted butter
2 teaspoon olive oil
2 garlic cloves, thinly sliced
1 bunch collard greens, trimmed, roughly chopped

Directions:
1. Put the ribs in a big pot and add cold water to cover them and 2 teaspoons of salt. Bring it to a boil over medium heat, and then turn it down to low. Simmer the ribs until they become tender, which will take around 45 minutes,

occasionally removing any scum from the surface. Move to a big wire rack placed on a tray and let them cool down.
2. Prepare barbecue sauce by heating the oil in a pan over medium heat. Put in the onion and garlic and cook for about 4 minutes. Add all the other ingredients for the sauce, and stir to mix. Simmer and cook for approximately 15 minutes, or until it gets thick. Strain through a fine sleeve in a dish and throw away any solids. Let it cool down.
3. Preheat your barbecue to medium heat. Coat the ribs with barbecue sauce and sprinkle with salt. Grill them for approximately 10-12 minutes, flipping and coating with sauce every 2 minutes.
4. To prepare the collard greens, warm the butter and oil in a large sauté pan over medium heat. Add the garlic and stir for approximately 1 minute. Put in the collard greens and stir for an additional 4-6 minutes until the collards are tender. Season with salt and pepper.
5. Serve warm with a side of coleslaw and some hot sauce if desired.

Caribbean's Barbecue Recipes

The Caribbean Grilled Chicken

This high-protein recipe for barbecued chicken originates from the Caribbean region and offers an exceptionally flavored marinade.

Serves: 4

Ingredients:
1 teaspoon allspice
¼ cup chopped red onion
½ cup chopped green onions
2 tablespoons extra-virgin olive oil
¼ cup fresh orange juice
1 tablespoon lime zest
2 tablespoons soy sauce
2 tablespoons thyme leaves, freshly chopped
2 tablespoons jalapeno chilies, seeded, diced
2 teaspoons freshly grated or chopped ginger
1 clove garlic
Salt and pepper
4 bone-in chicken breasts, skin on
Lime wedges

Directions:
1. To make the marinade, set aside the chicken and lime wedges and put all the remaining ingredients into a food processor. Puree them and then place the marinade, together with the chicken, in a plastic bag. Mix thoroughly until the chicken is nicely coated and then put it in the refrigerator for 4-8 hours.
2. You will need high heat on your grill. Once the grill is hot enough, drain any excess marinade and place the chicken on the grates.
3. Grill on each side for at least 5 minutes, or until they are nicely browned.

Traditional Drunken Grilled Chicken

Rum is one of the Caribbean trademarks and when you marinate the chicken in it, you get that beautiful flavor for your barbecue.

Serves: 6

Ingredients:
6 chicken breasts, wing bone in, skin on
Grilled corn on the cob, to serve

Marinade
½ cup lime juice
½ cup dark rum
½ cup dark soy sauce
1 small bunch thyme, leaves picked and coarsely chopped
1 long red chili, seeded and finely chopped
3 teaspoon grated palm sugar

Directions:
1. Prepare the marinade by mixing all the ingredients in an airtight container. Shake to combine.
2. Use a sharp knife to create 3 deep incisions in the chicken through its skin side. This will help the marinade to penetrate. Coat the chicken well in the marinade and refrigerate overnight. If you don't have time, cover with plastic wrap and let it rest for half an hour.
3. Preheat your grill to medium, take the chicken out of the marinade and place it on the barbecue. Cook for about 15 minutes, flipping and marinating it frequently. Let it rest for about 5 minutes before serving with grilled corn on the cob.

Spicy Pork Chops with Potatoes

Beautifully balanced flavors for the marinade and amazing potato salad create a total meal for your afternoon party or family gathering.

Serves: 4

Ingredients:
4 5-ounce pork chops, sliced
Lime wedges

Marinade
1 tablespoon black peppercorns
1 tablespoon allspice berries
½ teaspoon ground cinnamon
½ grated nutmeg
¼ bunch thyme
5 spring onions, chopped
3 garlic cloves, chopped
1 very hot chili, chopped
1 tablespoon dark brown sugar
2 tablespoons dark soy sauce
Juice of 1 lime
Sea salt

Sweet potato salad
4 sweet potatoes, cut in half
4 sprigs thyme
Freshly ground black pepper and sea salt
Olive oil
¼ red onion, chopped
1 large tomato, chopped
1 small bunch cilantro, chopped
1 small bunch flat-leaf parsley, chopped
1 lime
Freshly grated nutmeg, to taste

Directions:
1. Put the peppercorns and allspice berries in a blender and combine them with the cinnamon, nutmeg, thyme, spring onions, garlic, and chili. Process until smooth and then add the sugar, soy sauce, and lime juice. Transfer the mixture to a bowl, put in the pork, and massage the marinade into the meat. Season with a bit of salt and refrigerate for a minimum of 4 hours or overnight. Make sure to cover with wrap or a secure lid.
2. Prepare the sweet potato salad by putting a sprig of thyme between each half of the sweet potatoes. Drizzle with salt, a bit of oil, and wrap them in foil. Place them on a preheated barbecue and cook them.
3. Take out the pork and grill for 4 minutes per side.
4. Take the sweet potatoes off the barbecue and remove the thyme. Slice the potatoes roughly and season with salt and pepper. Add the chopped onion, tomato, and herbs. Squeezing the lime over the potatoes, and put in a nice grating of nutmeg.

Barbecued Chicken with Cilantro Salsa

This intensely flavored grilled chicken will be a real adventure for your mouth. The more time it spends in your fridge, the more it will soak up this intense flavor.

Serves: 8

Ingredients:
1 cup vegetable oil
1 large yellow onion, coarsely chopped
3 scallions, coarsely chopped
2 Scotch bonnet peppers, stem and seeds removed
2 tablespoons fresh ginger, grated
4 garlic cloves, chopped
2 tablespoons fresh thyme leaves, chopped
¼ cup red wine vinegar
1 tablespoon light brown sugar
¼ teaspoon freshly ground nutmeg
¼ teaspoon ground cinnamon
1 teaspoon ground allspice
½ teaspoon salt
Pinch ground cloves
¼ teaspoon black pepper, freshly grounded
2 tablespoons fresh lime juice
8 chicken thighs, skin on, bone in
8 drumsticks, skin on

For the mango and cilantro salsa
3 ripe mangoes, cut into dices
¼ cup red onion
2 tablespoons cilantro leaves, chopped
1 tablespoon oregano leaves, chopped
1 tablespoon green onions, chopped
3 tablespoons lime juice
3 tablespoons orange juice
1 teaspoon honey
Salt and freshly ground black pepper

Directions:
1. For the marinade, set aside the chicken, and mix all other ingredients in a food processor or blender until the mixture is almost smooth.
2. Make tiny holes in the chicken using a fork. Coat the chicken with the marinade. Cover with plastic wrap and put it in the refrigerator for 1-2 days.
3. Mix all ingredients for the salsa in one bowl and let it rest for about half an hour while you prepare the chicken.
4. Preheat your barbecue to a medium-high heat. Remove the chicken from the marinade and grill for approximately 5 minutes per side, or until cooked through. Let it rest for 5 minutes, and serve with a spoonful of salsa.

Shrimp Scampi Skewers with Mango Salsa

This beautiful and light summer barbecue recipe is great for when you get tired of traditional meat recipes.

Serves: 6

Ingredients:
18 large shrimp scampi, peeled with heads and tails intact, cleaned
6 bamboo skewers, soaked in water for 30 minutes
3 ripe mangoes, chopped
2 long red chilies, chopped
4 spring onions, sliced
4 shallots, chopped
1 bunch cilantro, stems and leaves chopped
1 bunch mint, leaves chopped
½ cup plus 2 tablespoons olive oil
¼ cup plus 2 tablespoons white wine vinegar

Directions:
1. Place 3 shrimp scampi on every skewer and place them in a bowl. Cover with wrap and put in the refrigerator.
2. Put the mango, chilies, spring onions, shallots, cilantro, mint, ⅓ cup of oil and ⅓ cup of vinegar in a blender. Pulse until roughly chopped, and season with salt and pepper if desired. Move half of the mixture to a bowl, and process the rest of it again with 2 tablespoons more of each vinegar and oil. Pour the mixture over the shrimp scampi and put into the refrigerator for approximately 2 hours.
3. Preheat your barbecue and grill for approximately 3-4 minutes per side or until cooked through. Serve with the salsa.

Backyard Barbecue Jerk Grilled Chicken

This recipe is often used in the Caribbean region, and it might be perfect for your backyard barbecue with your friends

Serves: 4-6

Ingredients:
1 whole free-range chicken (about 5 pounds), cut into 10 pieces
Limes, for garnish
Parsley, for garnish

For jerk marinade:
2 teaspoons allspice
½ teaspoon ground cinnamon
½ teaspoon ground nutmeg
½ onion
8 cloves garlic or 1 whole head
1 1-inch piece fresh ginger, sliced
3 spring onions, sliced
3 limes, juiced
Splash low-sodium soy sauce
¼ cup extra-virgin olive oil, plus more for drizzling
Salt and fresh ground pepper
6 sprigs fresh thyme, leaves picked
1 Scotch bonnet pepper, halved, plus more to taste
¼ cup packed light brown sugar

Directions:
1. Mix all the ingredients for the marinade in a food processor. Blend it until it becomes smooth.
2. Use a big plastic bag that you can reseal, and put the chicken pieces in it. Pour the marinade in, and turn to coat the chicken. Seal the bag and refrigerate overnight.
3. Preheat your barbecue to high heat. Grill each side of the chicken pieces until they are nicely browned. You can use vegetable oil to coat the chicken or the grates to prevent sticking. Serve with parsley and limes.

Caribbean Asado with Chimichurri

Try this amazing recipe from the Caribbean region and enjoy the delicious chimichurri sauce.

Serves 4-6

Ingredients:
Chimichurri
1 cup finely chopped flat-leaf parsley
3 garlic cloves, finely chopped
½ cup olive oil
3 tablespoons balsamic vinegar
3 tablespoons brown vinegar
½ teaspoon chili powder
1 teaspoon adobo spice mix
Salt

Asado meat
4 chorizo sausages
½ pound veal sweetbreads
4 pork chops, 1 inch-thick

Directions:
1. Preheat your grill on low heat and oil the grate. Cook the chorizo, sweetbread and pork chops for approximately an hour, or until cooked through.
2. Make the chimichurri by combining all ingredients in a blender.
3. Place the cooked mix meat on a serving plate and drizzle the chimichurri over the meat.

Barbecued Corn with Coconut Sauce

You can find coconuts all over the Caribbean, so it doesn't strike anyone as weird that coconut is an integral part of this vegetarian barbecue recipe.

Serves: 3-6

Ingredients:
6 cobs sweet corn, husks on
1 cup coconut cream or milk
2 tablespoons butter
1 teaspoon corn flour
¼ teaspoon salt
1 small bunch green onions (scallions), thinly sliced
1 ½ tablespoons freshly grated coconut or desiccated coconut

Directions:
1. Remove a couple of external layers of corn husk. Put the corn cobs on a preheated grill and grill them for 15-20 minutes, flipping periodically.
2. Put the coconut cream or milk, butter, corn flour, and salt in a small pan. Simmer for approximately 4 minutes, whisking regularly. Add the coconut and spring onion and take it off the heat.
3. Peel back the corn husks and remove the silks. Brush with coconut sauce and place them back on the grill. Grill for an additional 2 minutes, basting with sauce and flipping frequently. Serve with the remaining sauce.

Cuban Spicy Mojo Chicken

You can choose to eat this cold or hot, but Mojo chicken is ideal with orange and lime wedges either way.

Serves: 4-6

Ingredients:
1 whole chicken, about 4 pounds, cut into 10 pieces
Lime and orange wedges, for garnish
Black beans and rice, to serve

Mojo marinade
2 cloves garlic
1 long red chili, chopped
1 teaspoon salt
2 oranges, 1 zested, 1 juiced
2 limes, juiced
1 teaspoon dried oregano
1 teaspoon ground cumin
2 tablespoons olive oil

Directions:
1. Use a mortar and pestle to pound the garlic, chili, and 1 teaspoon of salt. Mix in the orange juice and zest, lime juice, oregano, cumin, and oil.
2. Use a sharp knife to score the meat, and then coat it well with the marinade. Put it into the refrigerator overnight.
3. Preheat your barbecue to medium heat. Take the meat out of the marinade and arrange it on the grate. Grill until it is cooked, making sure to turn occasionally.
4. Serve with black beans and rice, garnished with lime and orange wedges.

South America's Barbecue Recipes

Barbecued Pork Skewers with Melon Salad

A great combination of spices, as well as melon salad and grilled cheese, which are served alongside this pork.

Serves: 6

Ingredients:
1 ½ pounds boneless pork leg, cut into cubes
2 limes, juiced
4 garlic cloves, peeled and smashed
1 teaspoon ground black pepper
½ teaspoon hot smoked paprika
2 tablespoons olive oil
2 blocks halloumi cheese
1 tablespoon whole grain mustard
3 tablespoons honey
Sea salt flakes

For the salad
1 ripe honeydew melon, cut into cubes after previously deseeded
1 cucumber, seeded and diced
1 red chili, nicely sliced
Small bunch mint, sliced
2 limes, juice
Lime wedges

Directions:
1. In a large bowl, combine the lime juice, garlic, pepper, paprika, and oil. Add the pork, and stir to coat the meat. Put a cover over it and place it in the refrigerator for at least 2 hours (but no more than 3). In the meantime, soak some bamboo skewers in a pot of cold water.

2. Heat a barbecue to a high heat. Mix the mustard and honey in a separate bowl and put it aside. Thread the pork on the skewers, season with salt, and grill on each side for about 3 minutes. Baste from time to time with the honey-mustard mixture. Transfer the cooked skewers to a serving platter and let them cool.
3. Slice the cheese in half lengthwise to create four rectangles. Put them on skewers and grill each side for about two minutes until it becomes crisp.
4. In the meantime, mix the ingredients for the salad. You can season it to your liking. Now when you have it all prepared, serve the skewers with melon salad, grilled cheese and lime wedges.

Flathead Fish Fillets

A perfect recipe for your outdoor barbecue. A beautiful salsa will add to the flavor.

Serves: 6

Ingredients:
1 ½ pounds flathead (or other firm white fish) fillets, cut into ¾-inch dices
3 tablespoons olive oil
Juice of 1 lime
20 soft white corn tortillas, 4 inches in diameter

Salsa
2 garlic cloves, peeled and crushed
1 green pepper, seeded and finely diced
6 roma (plum) tomatoes, seeded and chopped
1 small red (Spanish) onion, finely diced
1-2 small red or green chilies, finely sliced
6 cilantro stalks, including roots, well washed
Pepper
1 teaspoon salt
2 tablespoons extra-virgin olive oil
Juice of 1 lime
Lemon juice, to serve

Fish spice
2 teaspoons fennel seeds
2 teaspoons coriander (cilantro seeds)
2 teaspoons cumin seeds
¾ teaspoon salt
1-2 teaspoons chipotle powder or similar chili powder

Directions:
1. Prepare the salsa by mixing the garlic, pepper, tomatoes, onion, and sliced chilies. Chop the cilantro, and add the roots and stems, setting the leaves aside. Mix well. Let it rest for about 30 minutes.

2. Use a mortar and pestle to pound the fennel, coriander, cumin seeds, and ¾ teaspoon of salt. Add the chipotle powder, and sprinkle the mixture over the fish to coat. Let it rest 10-20 minutes to absorb the flavors.
3. Finish the salsa by adding pepper, 1 teaspoon of salt, extra virgin oil, lime juice and the cilantro leaves. Combine well.
4. Oil the grates and heat the barbecue to medium heat, about 350°F. Place a foil sheet on the grill. Brush it with olive oil. Place the fish cubes on the foil paper. Grill for 4-8 minutes, stirring gently the fish a few times until the fish is cooked through. Sprinkle lemon juice over it. Transfer to a plate and cover loosely with foil to keep warm.
5. Warm up the tortillas on the barbecue, about 20 seconds on each side.
6. To serve, assemble the tortillas with some of the fish and a generous scoop of salsa and roll it up.

Grilled Cheese Stuffed Chicken Breasts

Uruguayans are famous for making good barbecue. This is an unconventional chicken recipe for anyone who wants to make something exquisite.

Serves: 4

Ingredients:
4 chicken breasts
1 lime
2 tablespoons salt
1 red bell pepper
½ cup cream cheese, softened, divided
½ cup chimichurri sauce, divided
4 slices deli ham
8 ounces mozzarella cheese, cubed
4 green onions, chopped
¼ cup sliced green or black olives
16 slices bacon
Salt and freshly ground black pepper

Directions:
1. Put the chicken in a bowl and pour cold water over it. Squeeze in the juice of 1 lime, and 2 tablespoons of salt. Refrigerate for a minimum of 2 hours, ideally overnight.
2. Grill the red pepper until it is blackened. Let it cool down and then remove the burned skin. Take out the seeds and cut it into strips, each being a ½-inch wide.
3. Mix ¼ cup of the chimichurri sauce with cream cheese.
4. Take the chicken out of the marinade, season with salt and pepper and cut each breast in half horizontally — but not all the way through. Open the meat outwards, place a piece of plastic wrap over it, put it on chopping board and pound it with a mallet.
5. Remove the wrap and drizzle 2 tablespoons of the cream cheese mixture over it. Place two strips of roasted pepper and a piece of deli ham on the cream cheese. Sprinkle ¼ of each of the cheese cubes, green onions, and sliced olives on the ham.

Finish each with a bacon slice set to one edge of every breast. Roll the chicken and close up the filling. Wrap the additional bacon around the outside of the rolls.
6. Wrap each roll in foil and place on a preheated barbecue. Grill for approximately 20 minutes, then remove the foil and place the meat back on the barbecue. Continue cooking until it is cooked through.

Barbecued Pork Belly

The amazing thing about this Chilean recipe is that it is extremely easy to prepare and gives excellent results.

Serves: 1

Ingredients:
6 garlic cloves, roughly chopped
⅓ cup salt
¼ cup dried oregano
1 tablespoon sweet paprika
2 tablespoons smoked paprika
½ cup ground cumin
1 ¾ ounces merquen
5 ounces white wine vinegar
4 ½ pounds pork belly, excess fat trimmed, ribs still attached and split down the middle (but not all the way through)

Directions:
1. In a pan, heat the olive oil and sear the outside of the meat. Set it aside.
2. Use a mortar and pestle to pound the garlic and salt.
3. In a mixing bowl, combine the ground garlic and salt with the oregano, paprika, cumin, and merquen. Gradually add the vinegar.
4. Use a sharp knife to remove any skin and fat from the pork belly (or ask your butcher). Score the fat side and in between the ribs. Rub well with the marinade and refrigerate for at least one night (to a maximum 3 days).
5. Take out the meat and bring it to room temperature. Take out the pork belly, but keep the marinade.
6. Cook over coals and baste periodically with the reserved marinade. Make sure to turn occasionally and after a while, split the ribs down the center before continuing with cooking. Do not baste in the final minutes of cooking, to allow the final application of marinade to cook.

Asado Beef Ribs with Wine Marinade

The term asado means that pieces of meat should be ready for grilling. In this Argentinian recipe, you need asado beef ribs, which taste great when marinated with wine.

Serves: 18

Ingredients:
4 ½ pounds asado beef ribs
1 ½ cups dry red wine
1 ½ tablespoons medium-grain salt

Directions:
1. Mix the beef ribs with the wine and allow it to marinate for about 10-20 minutes. Drain the marinade and then use salt to coat the ribs.
2. Preheat your barbecue to medium. Grill the beef ribs until they are cooked, flipping from time to time.

Argentinian Skewers with Steak Sauce

If you and your friends are fans of medium-rare beef and an excellent steak sauce, this is a perfect combination for you.

Serves: 4

Ingredients:
<u>For the beef skewers</u>
¼ cup fresh cilantro leaves
2 heads garlic, exterior peeled and cut in half horizontally
2 jalapeno peppers, tops removed
¼ cup fresh flat-leaf parsley
¼ cup canola oil, plus some for grilling
18 ounces beef sirloin, cut into 1-inch cubes
Wooden skewers
Freshly ground black salt and pepper
12 spring onions

<u>For the sherry vinegar steak sauce</u>
4 piquillo peppers, chopped (or 2 roasted red peppers, chopped)
½ cup mature sherry vinegar
3 tablespoons Dijon mustard
1 tablespoon drained horseradish
3 tablespoons honey
1 ½ tablespoons molasses
2 teaspoons Worcestershire sauce
1 teaspoon salt
½ teaspoon freshly ground black pepper

Directions:
1. Mix the cilantro, garlic, peppers, parsley, and oil in a food processor until they become smooth. Move the mixture to a big bowl, put in the beef and make sure it is nicely coated with the mixture. Put a cover over it and put it in the refrigerator for at least half an hour and at most, 8 hours.
2. Preheat your barbecue to high heat. Put the beef on skewers and season it with salt and pepper. Grill it until it is medium-rare, usually not more than 3 minutes on each side.

3. Brush the spring onions with canola oil and grill them for about two minutes on each side. You can also season them with salt and pepper if desired.
4. To make the sauce, mix the peppers, vinegar, mustard, horseradish, honey, molasses, Worcestershire, salt, and pepper in a food processor. Process it until it becomes smooth. It is recommended for the sauce to be made a day in advance and stored in the refrigerator.

Churrasco de Picanha with Brown Butter

Rock salt is mandatory when it comes to preparing picanha in Brazil. Brown herb butter is an optional addition, but I believe you will appreciate it

Serves: 12 and more

Ingredients:
3 rump caps (around 2 ½ pounds each), excess fat and sinew removed from the underside, cut into 1-inch cubes (also known as beef top sirloin caps)
Rock salt

Brown herb butter (optional)
1 pound salted butter, cubed
A handful of fresh rosemary and thyme sprigs, leaves picked

Tomato and onion vinaigrette
3 ½ pounds tomatoes, finely chopped
2 red onions, finely chopped
1 bunch chopped flat-leaf (Italian) parsley
⅓ cup red wine vinegar
1 cup extra-virgin olive oil

Directions:
1. Prepare the grill to medium high heat. If using charcoals, wait until the coals turn white before cooking. Let the beef reach room temperature before skewing the beef onto the spit.
2. Mix all the ingredients for the tomato and onion vinaigrette in a big bowl, and put in a pinch of salt. Combine well. Set aside.
3. In a pan, melt the butter and cook it until it becomes brown. Mix in the herbs and take it off the heat.
4. When ready to cook, massage the beef with the rock salt and brush with brown butter.
5. Cook on the spit for 20 to 30 minutes until the beef is cooked to your desired level of doneness.

6. As the meat cooks, cut layers off and baste the outside of the roasts with brown butter once again. Continue grilling until the crust is formed again.
7. Serve with some of the tomato and onions vinaigrette.

Barbecued Chivito

Chivito is what a goat is called in Argentina, and grilled chivito is one of the local specialties, which has now found its way to your backyard.

Serves: 20

Ingredients:
8 cloves of garlic
1 lemon, juiced
¼ cup white vinegar
¼ cup olive oil
2 teaspoons ground cumin
2 teaspoons sweet paprika
1 teaspoon ground chili
3 teaspoons dried oregano
5 pounds goat meat, chopped into large pieces

Directions:
1. Grind the garlic and 2 tablespoons of salt in a pestle and mortar. In a large bowl, combine all the other ingredients with this mixture. Finally, add the goat meat to the marinade and coat it nicely. Cover and put in the refrigerator for at least 2 hours, ideally overnight.
2. Take out the goat from the refrigerator approximately an hour before grilling.
3. Preheat your barbecue to medium. Grill the goat until it is cooked to your taste, brushing it occasionally with the marinade that remained. Do not baste in the final few minutes of cooking, so the marinade will cook through.

Matambre Beef with Cheese

Matambre is what they call a steak in Argentina when it is stuffed with blue cheese and pepper.

Serves: 4

Ingredients:
1 flank steak, about 1 ½ pounds, 1-inch thick
1 tablespoon grated Parmesan
2 teaspoons sweet paprika
1 tablespoon oregano
½ red pepper, cut into thin strips
1 onion, thinly sliced
2 garlic cloves, finely chopped
¼ cup blue cheese, crumbled
⅓ cup heavy cream
¼ cup green olives, pitted, sliced
½ cup prosciutto, thinly sliced

Directions:
1. Place the flank steak with the fat-side down on a cutting board. Use a sharp knife to cut the steak horizontally in half, not cutting all the way through, and open up the flank. Sprinkle Parmesan, paprika, and oregano over it and season to taste with salt and pepper. On one half, place the pepper, onion, garlic, blue cheese, cream, olives, and prosciutto. Fold the flank and sew the edges together using a needle and thread.
2. Preheat the barbecue to medium-high. Place the folded and stuffed flank on the barbecue. Grill until it is cooked through or to your liking, making sure to turn occasionally. Let it cool down for about 5 minutes and slice.

Asia's Barbecue Recipes

Farro Salad with Sherry Vinaigrette

This salad recipe that comes from Asia might be ideal for vegetarians, or as a side for your main course.

Serves: 4-6

Ingredients:
8 ounces farro
3 Japanese (baby) eggplants, halved
1 small red onion, peeled, halved, and thickly sliced
Olive oil, for brushing
Salt and freshly ground black pepper
¾ cup cherry tomatoes, washed and halved
4 tablespoons chopped fresh dill, plus more for garnish
Sherry Vinaigrette, recipe follows

For the sherry vinaigrette
1 small shallot, finely chopped
¼ cup sherry vinegar or balsamic vinegar
2 teaspoons Dijon mustard
¼ teaspoon salt
¼ teaspoon freshly ground black pepper
4 tablespoons chopped fresh dill
½ cup olive oil

Directions:
1. Cook the farro in a large pot of salted boiling water for about 15 minutes, until it becomes tender. Drain it, and transfer it to a big bowl.
2. Preheat the barbecue to high. Coat the onion slices and eggplants with oil and grill for approximately 4 minutes per side. Take them off the grate and cut into 1-inch pieces.
3. In a small bowl, combine the ingredients for the sherry vinaigrette.

4. Mix the cooked eggplant and onions into the farro, as well as the tomatoes and dill. Sprinkle sherry vinaigrette over it, and mix to combine.

Vietnamese Grilled Pork with Noodles

If you want to try something different, yet tasteful, make sure to give this wonderful Vietnamese traditional meal a chance.

Serves: 4

Ingredients:
2 tablespoons sugar
4 tablespoons fish sauce
1 tablespoon honey
1 teaspoon freshly ground pepper
2 cloves garlic, finely diced
6 spring onions, (white part only) finely sliced and mashed well in a mortar and pestle
18 ounces pork neck, finely sliced across the grain into 3mm pieces
2 tablespoons vegetable oil
1 cup rice vermicelli noodles (cooked according to packet instructions)
1 Lebanese cucumber, halved and sliced
5 Vietnamese mint leaves, sliced
5 perilla leaves, sliced
5 mint leaves, sliced
2 handfuls bean sprouts
½ cup fish sauce for dipping
4 tablespoons shallot oil
4 tablespoons crushed roasted peanuts

Directions:
1. In a large bowl, mix the sugar, fish sauce, honey, and pepper. Stir until the sugar has dissolved and then put in the garlic, mashed spring onion, and sliced pork neck.
2. Coat the pork well with the mixture, then with vegetable oil. Refrigerate it for at least 2 hours, but preferably overnight.
3. Put the pork on skewers and preheat your grill to a medium-high heat. Grill the skewers for approximately 2 minutes per side.

4. Cooked the vermicelli noodles and divide them into 4 bowls. In each, put some cucumber, some of the sliced mints, and bean sprouts. Divide the pork skewers among the bowls. Use 1-2 tablespoons of fish sauce to garnish each bowl, as well as a little shallot oil and crushed peanuts.

Spicy Chicken Kebabs with Papaya Salad

This kebab recipe comes from Thailand, so it shouldn't come as a surprise that it includes papaya for that additional flavor boost.

Serves:4-6

Ingredients:
2 large boneless chicken breasts, cubed

Marinade
2 jalapenos chilies
1 lemongrass, chopped
1 inch- fresh ginger piece, grated
1 garlic clove, minced
1 teaspoon lime zest
2 tablespoons soy sauce
1 tablespoon fish sauce

Side Salad
2 carrots, peeled
1 papaya, peeled
1 cup baby spinach
12 Cherry tomatoes
1 cup cooked green beans, cut into 1-inch lengths
1 tablespoon sesame oil
2 tablespoon olive oil
4 green onions, sliced
1 tablespoon rice vinegar
1 tablespoon Thai chile sauce
1 tablespoon soy sauce
1 tablespoon fresh lime juice
1 tablespoon fresh cilantro, chopped
1 tablespoons mint leaves, chopped

Roasted nuts for garnish

Directions:
1. Whisk all the marinade ingredients together in a medium bowl. Add the chicken and stir to coat well. Cover with plastic wrap and marinate for at least 30 minutes up to 2 hours in the refrigerator.
2. Chop the carrots and papaya into fine strips. Put them in a large bowl with the spinach, cherry tomatoes and green onions.
3. Mix the remaining ingredients together in a small bowl.
4. Put the pork on skewers. Prepare your grill and cook the chicken until it is nicely browned on each side.

Barbecued Prawns with Garlic and Soy Sauce

If you're in the mood for grilled prawns, the marinade they prepare in Asia might give you an even better meal.

Serves: 4

Ingredients:
¼ cup plus 1 teaspoon soy sauce
2 limes, juiced
2 tablespoons plus 2 teaspoons toasted sesame oil
2 teaspoons honey
2 2-inch pieces fresh ginger, finely grated
4 cloves garlic, finely chopped
½ cup rapeseed oil divided
½ cup butter, softened
2 ½ cups large prawns, peeled and deveined

Directions:
1. Mix ¼ cup of soy sauce, the lime juice, 2 tablespoons of sesame oil, honey, ginger, garlic, and ¼ cup of rapeseed oil. Put the mixture into a food processor, add the butter, and blend until it is nicely combined.
2. Season the prawns with salt and pepper, and coat with the sauce.
3. Prepare your grill and cook the prawns on each side for approximately 2 minutes.

Traditional Indian Lamb Skewers

What makes these skewers special is the dipping sauce you prepare with it, which includes yogurt, garlic and mint.

Serves: 8

Ingredients:
2 pounds pack lean minced lamb
1 onion, finely chopped
3 tablespoons curry paste
1 small bunch cilantro, chopped
½ cup fat-free yogurt
2 tablespoons chopped mint
1 clove garlic, crushed
½ cup bagged herb salad
2 pieces Indian-style bread, such as naan

Directions:
1. In a medium bowl, mix the lamb, onion, curry paste, and most of the chopped cilantro. Form the lamb into long patties and put it on the skewers.
2. Preheat your grill to a medium-high heat and grill the lamb until it is cooked through.
3. Combine the yogurt, mint, and garlic in a small bowl and warm up the bread on your grill. Serve with a handful of the herb salad, and the rest of the cilantro.

Sweet Asian Barbecued Salmon

Completely change the taste of your grilled salmon with special barbecue sauce they prepare in Asia.

Serves: 4

Ingredients:
2 tablespoons canola oil, plus more for grilling
2 shallots, sliced (about 2 tablespoons)
1 teaspoon garlic, chopped
¼ cup hoisin sauce
¼ cup tomato ketchup
2 tablespoons honey
1 tablespoon sambal oelek
2-3 tablespoons sesame seeds, toasted
1 teaspoon soy sauce
1 teaspoon fish sauce
1 tablespoon rice vinegar
Salt and freshly ground black pepper
4 (8-ounce) salmon steaks
Cilantro leaves, for garnish

Directions:
1. Heat the oil in a small pan over a medium heat. Put in the garlic and shallots and cook until they become soft. Add the hoisin sauce, ketchup, honey, sambal oelek, sesame seeds, soy sauce, and fish sauce, and cook for additional 5 minutes. Take it off the heat and add the vinegar. Season to your liking with salt and pepper.
2. Preheat your barbecue to high heat. Oil the salmon on each side and season with salt and pepper if desired. Grill to a medium-well doneness, making sure to baste it with the sauce regularly.
3. Transfer the fish to a platter and put more sauce on it. Let it cool down for 5 minutes and serve garnished with cilantro.

Classic Chicken Asian Skewers

This nice Asian marinade will give your skewers a great flavor. You can serve them with your favorite dipping sauce.

Serves: 4

Ingredients:
3 tablespoons cilantro leaves
¼ cup vegetable oil
1 tablespoon Asian hot chili sauce
1 tablespoon light brown sugar
2 teaspoons soy sauce
1-2 cloves garlic
One 2-inch chunk fresh ginger, peeled and roughly chopped
1 small onion, roughly chopped
Sea salt
1 pound boneless, skinless chicken thighs, cut into 12 4-inch strips
Dipping sauce (to serve), such as cilantro chutney, sweet chili sauce or ponzu sauce

Directions:
1. In a food processor, combine the cilantro, oil, chili sauce, sugar, soy sauce, garlic, ginger, onions and a half a teaspoon of salt. Blend until smooth.
2. Put the chicken on skewers, and arrange them in a baking dish. Coat them with the marinade and refrigerate them for about 2 hours.
3. Preheat your grill to medium-high heat. Take the skewers out of the baking dish and throw away the marinade. Grill the chicken for approximately 5 minutes on each side, until it is cooked through.

Traditional Korean Ribs

It might be a nice idea to look for kimchi, a kind of spicy pickled cabbage which is eaten in Korea with this meal.

Serves: 20

Ingredients:
1 cup soy sauce
½ cup mirin (sweet Japanese rice wine) or sweet sherry
¾ cup (packed) dark brown sugar
¼ cup rice vinegar
2 tablespoons sesame oil
2 tablespoons minced garlic
¼ cup water
2 large green onions, chopped
5 pounds Korean-style short ribs (
Cooked spinach, for serving

Directions:
1. Mix the soy sauce, mirin, brown sugar, rice vinegar, sesame oil, minced garlic, and green onions in a bowl and stir to combine them well. Use a big re-sealable plastic bag and pour the mixture into it. Add the ribs and seal the bag. Coat the ribs nicely and put them in the refrigerator for at least 8 hours up to 12 hours.
2. Preheat your barbecue to medium-high heat. Take out the ribs and discard the marinade. Grill the ribs to medium-rare, approximately 3-4 minutes on each side. For a meat well done, grill 5-7 minutes per side.
3. Serve with spinach.

Barbecued Caipirinha Skewers

Since caipirinha is actually a famous Brazilian cocktail, this might not be recipe for kids. However, it is perfect for a party with your friends.

Serves: 4-6

Ingredients:
2 bunches of mint, leaves picked, plus extra to serve
1 cup lime juice, plus 2 tablespoons for serving
1 lime, zested
½ cup cachaça
2 long red chilies, finely chopped
1 tablespoon brown sugar
¼ cup olive oil
¼ teaspoon cayenne pepper
1 pound boneless chicken thigh, trimmed, cut into 1-inch pieces
Wooden skewers, soaked in water for 30 minutes

Directions:
1. Chop half a cup of mint, and put it in a bowl. Mix in the lime juice, lime zest, cachaça, chilies, sugar, oil, and cayenne. Season it to taste with salt and pepper and mix well. Set aside ⅓ of the marinade for basting, and mix the chicken with the remaining ⅔. Coat the meat well and refrigerate for one night.
2. Take the chicken out of the marinade and thread it on skewers, alternating with the mint you have remaining. Place the skewers on the barbecue and grill for approximately 8 minutes, turning periodically and basting with the remaining marinade. Sprinkle with a little extra lime juice and serve with mojo and extra mint.

Spicy Chicken Satay with Peanut Sauce

Original barbecue recipe coming from Eastern Asia with piquant dipping sauce.

Serves: 4

Ingredients:
½ cup low-sodium chicken stock
½ cup light coconut milk
2 tablespoons low sodium soy sauce
1 shallot, sliced thin
1 clove garlic, minced
1 ½ teaspoons Thai fish sauce (or 2 additional teaspoons of low sodium soy sauce)
1 tablespoon brown sugar
½ teaspoon lime zest
1 tablespoon minced fresh ginger
1 pound boneless, skinless, chicken breast, pounded slightly and cut into 1-inch strips
¾ cup spicy peanut dipping sauce, recipe below
3 tablespoons chopped toasted peanuts
2 tablespoons minced fresh basil or cilantro leaves

For the spicy peanut dipping sauce
¼ cup natural creamy peanut butter
¼ cup low sodium chicken broth
3 tablespoons low sodium soy sauce
1 ½ tablespoons brown sugar
1 ½ tablespoons minced fresh ginger
2 tablespoons lime juice
1 teaspoon minced garlic
½ teaspoon chili flakes
1 teaspoon curry paste
1 shallot, peeled and roughly chopped

Directions:
1. In one bowl, mix together the chicken stock, coconut milk, soy sauce, shallot, garlic, fish sauce, sugar, lime zest, and ginger. Stir in the chicken strips and leave it to marinate for an hour. Take the chicken out of the marinade and throw the marinade away.
2. Preheat your grill to medium-high heat. Put the chicken onto the skewers and barbecue it for a couple of minutes on each side, until it is cooked through.
3. Prepare the peanut dipping sauce by putting all the ingredients for it in a food processor and pureeing it until smooth. You can keep the sauce refrigerated for 3 or 4 days.
4. Serve the chicken with the sauce, garnished with chopped peanuts and cilantro.

Grilled Salmon with Masala Salsa

This salmon brings the refreshing taste of India to your own backyard family barbecue.

Serves: 2

Ingredients:
For the mango masala salsa
8 ounces chopped ripe mango
1 ½ cup minced red onion
1 tablespoon minced cilantro
Pinch of garam masala
Pinch of salt
Few grinds of pepper
⅛ cup mango juice
Juice of half a lime

For the salmon
2 tablespoons curry leaves
1 tablespoon brown mustard seeds
½ teaspoon asafetida
2 tablespoons garam masala
2 5 ½-ounce salmon fillets, skin on
1 tablespoon grapeseed oil
Pinch of salt

Directions:
1. Put all the ingredients for the mango masala salsa in a bowl, cover it and put it in the refrigerator for about half an hour.
2. Put the curry leaves, mustard seeds, and asafetida in a pestle and mortar and make sure to grind it well. Put in the garam masala and grind it a couple more times.
3. Prepare your grill by getting it to a medium-high heat. Rub each fillet with oil, and season to your liking with salt and the spices. Make sure to gently oil the grate and place the salmon fillets on it. Grill for about 5 minutes on each side, making sure to brush it with oil when turning to the other side. To serve, top with some of the mango masala salsa.

Barbecued Salmon with Honey and Lime

You don't need any expert skills to prepare this recipe, and a combination of sweet honey and sour lime is a great addition to your salmon.

Serves: 4

Ingredients:
2 tablespoons cilantro leaves
2 spring onions
2 teaspoons vegetable oil
1 teaspoon ginger, grated
Salt and freshly ground pepper
4 center cut skin-on wild salmon fillets, about 6 ounces each
2 teaspoons fresh lime juice
2 teaspoons low-sodium soy sauce
2 teaspoons honey
¼ teaspoon black sesame seeds
12 ounces cooked edamame
Lime wedges, optional, for garnish

Directions:
1. Prepare your grill by bringing it to medium-high heat. Make sure to oil the grates.
2. Chop the cilantro into small pieces, and mix it with the onions, oil, and ginger.
3. Make two slits, each 4 inches in length, through the skin of the salmon fillets. The cuts need to be made on the bottom, lengthwise. Fill those slits with the herbal mixture. Season the salmon with salt and pepper.
4. Combine the lime juice, soy sauce, and honey. Place the salmon on the grill (the skin side should be up) and grill until nicely marked (3-4 minutes). Turn to the other side and brush the tops with the sauce before letting it grill for another 3-4 minutes on the other side.
5. Move the fish to a serving dish and sprinkle sesame seeds on tops. Serve with lime wedges and edamame.

Korean-style Barbecued Chicken

If you've ever wondered about the way chicken is grilled in Korea, why don't you try this recipe and see for yourself? You will surely be thrilled.

Serves: 4-6

Ingredients:
3 tablespoons rice vinegar
1 cup soy sauce
2 tablespoons honey
1 tablespoon Korean chili paste
2 tablespoons fresh ginger, grated
6 garlic cloves, crushed
1 spring onion, finely sliced
2 teaspoons toasted sesame oil
Freshly ground black pepper
1 ½ teaspoons toasted sesame seeds
1 3-pound chicken, butterflied
4 (6-inch) flour tortillas, warmed

Directions:
1. Mix the vinegar, soy sauce, honey, chili paste, ginger, and garlic in a medium bowl and divide it into two bowls.
2. Place the chicken pieces in a large bowl, and pour one portion of the sauce over. Mix to coat well. Cover with plastic wrap and refrigerate for a minimum of 4 hours and a maximum of 8 hours.
3. To the other portion, add the spring onion, sesame oil, pepper, and sesame seeds. Set this aside to use as a dipping sauce after you have grilled the chicken.
4. Preheat your grill to medium-high heat, but make sure to have a zone where there is indirect heat. Take the chicken out of the refrigerator and out of the marinade and place it on the grates. The skin side should be turned down. Grill it for approximately 10 minutes, then move it to the indirect heat, where it should stay until it is nicely cooked.

5. Transfer it to a cutting board and let it rest for 5 minutes before cutting it into portions and removing the bones. Wrap the meat in tortillas, arrange them on a plate and serve with dipping sauce.

Barbecued Scallops and Eggplant

This traditional Japanese starter is ideal for your family barbecue.

Serves 4-6

Ingredients:
2-3 Japanese eggplants
1 pounds scallops, rinsed
2 green onions, chopped, for garnish
Sesame seeds for garnish

Glaze
⅓ cup Chinese five-spice powder
½ shallot, finely chopped
1 clove garlic, minced
3 tablespoons light soy sauce
1 tablespoon rice vinegar
1 tablespoon hoisin sauce
⅓ cup ketchup
2 heaping tablespoons honey
2 heaping tablespoons apricot preserves
2 heaping tablespoons brown sugar
1 teaspoon freshly grated ginger
1 ½ teaspoons chili hot sauce, such as Sriracha

Directions:
1. Mix all the ingredients for the glaze in a saucepan. Bring to a boil on medium-high heat. Remove from heat and let cool down.
2. Prepare your grill by bringing it to high heat and oiling the grates. Cut the eggplant on the bias into ½-inch thick slices. Grill for approximately 3 minutes per side.
3. Brush some of the glaze on the cooked part of the eggplant, then flip to cook an additional minute while you brush the other side. Take it off the grill and put on a plate. Cover loosely with foil to keep warm.
4. Repeat the procedure with scallops. Arrange eggplants and scallop on a serving plate. Sprinkle with green onions and sesame seeds.

Thai-style Barbecued Beef Salad

Although this Thai recipe is imagined as a side dish, you can also use it as a light main course.

Serves: 4

Ingredients:
1 pound top-round London grill or flank steak, about 1 ½ inches thick
3 tablespoons low-sodium soy sauce
3 tablespoons lime juice, divided
3 tablespoons canola oil
2 tablespoons brown sugar
1 teaspoon minced garlic
1 ½ teaspoons minced ginger
1 ¼ teaspoons red curry paste or chili garlic sauce
½ head red-leaf lettuce, torn (about 6 cups)
½ cup cilantro leaves, rinsed and dried
1 cup basil leaves, sliced into ribbons
3 shallots, thinly sliced (about ½ cup), divided, for garnish

Directions:
1. Place the meat in a resealable plastic bag.
2. Mix the soy sauce, a tablespoon of lime juice, canola oil, brown sugar, garlic, ginger, and red curry paste in a bowl. Once you combine it well, pour one half in the bag with the meat, and add another tablespoon of lime juice to it. Refrigerate it for a minimum of 4 hours, or preferably overnight. Keep the other half of the mixture in your refrigerator to use as salad dressing.
3. Oil the grates of your barbecue and preheat it to medium heat. Grill the beef until it is medium-rare, and leave it to cool down at the room temperature. Once it cools down, slice it thin.
4. Mix the lettuce, cilantro, basil, and beef in a bowl. Add the dressing and toss to coat the salad. Divide the salad onto 4 plates, and garnish with shallots.

Tandoori Vegetarian Kebabs

Spicy flavors from this Tandoori paste are soothed by the yogurt. You will enjoy this carefully prepared Middle Eastern recipe.

Serves: 4-8

Ingredients:
1 cup paneer, cut into 1 ½-inch cubes
⅔ cup fried tofu puffs cut into 1 ½-inch pieces
⅔ cup cassava (or potato), peeled, cut into 1 ½-inch pieces and boiled until al dente
4 ounces baby button mushrooms, wiped clean

For the tandoori paste
1 teaspoon whole coriander (seeds)
6 black peppercorns
2 dried Kashmiri chilies
2 teaspoons fine cornmeal
1 1-inch piece of cassia bark
1 ½ teaspoons cumin seeds
1 star anise pod
4 cloves
Seeds of 4 cardamom pods
5 tablespoons tomato paste
3 cloves garlic, crushed
2 teaspoons ginger, peeled and minced
2 tablespoons dark brown sugar/muscovado sugar
Juice of 2 lemons
2-3 teaspoons salt, or to taste
1 tablespoon plain Greek yogurt

Directions:
1. To prepare the paste, mix the coriander, peppercorns, Kashmiri chilies, cornmeal, cassia bark, cumin, star anise, and cloves in a dry frying pan. Slowly toast them on low heat, while regularly moving them around in the pan.

2. Put them in a blender and process them until they are smooth. Add the tomato paste, garlic, ginger, sugar, lemon juice, salt, and yogurt, and process them again. You can optionally add a couple of tablespoons of water.
3. Put cubed paneer and tofu in a pan with boiling salted water, boil for 4 minutes, and then drain. Mix these with the cassava and mushrooms, and then combine with the tandoori paste. Put it in the refrigerator for at least 1 hour, to a maximum of 24 hours.
4. Place the pieces on skewers and arrange them on your grill. Barbecue them for a couple of minutes per side, until you see they are nicely charred.

Miso Chicken Skewers

The Japanese prepare these skewers with their traditional and tasteful basting sauce.

Serves: 8

Ingredients:
24 wooden skewers, soaked for 30 minutes in water then drained
2 pounds ground chicken, preferably thigh meat
6 green onions, trimmed and very finely chopped
¼ cup red miso
1 tablespoon sesame oil
Mizuna leaves, lime wedges and steamed rice for serving

Basting sauce
½ cup chicken stock
¼ cup mirin
¼ cup light soy sauce
2 tablespoons sake
1 ½ tablespoons caster sugar
1 clove of garlic, chopped
2 teaspoons ginger, finely grated

Directions:
1. To make the basting sauce, put all the ingredients in a pan or a wok and bring it to a simmer. Cook over medium heat for about 10 minutes or until reduced by half.
2. Place the ground chicken, green onions, miso, and sesame oil in a bowl. Season with salt and pepper to your liking, and mix together. Using your fingers, work the mixture for 5 minutes or until smooth and slightly elastic.
3. Split the mixture into 24 even-sized pieces and roll each into a ball. Wetting your hands regularly, shape the balls into a slightly flattened, oval blocks, about 5 inches long and 1 inch wide. Thread a skewer through each one.

4. Preheat a chargrill plate or a barbecue to medium. Coat the skewers lightly with marinade and then cook. Turn the skewers around from time to time and reapply the marinade. Barbecue for 5-6 minutes, or until just cooked through.
5. Arrange on a plate with steamed rice, and garnish with mizuna leaves and lime wedges, in the traditional Japanese way.

Adana-style Kebab

If you have ever gone to Turkey, you might know that every region has its own way of making kebabs. The way they're made in Adana is one of the most famous.

Serves: 4

Ingredients:
1 ½ pounds leg of lamb or lamb shoulder, boneless
7 ounces lamb fat (tail, bunting or kidney fat preferred)
1 red bell pepper or 2 red bullhorn peppers, cubed
2 tablespoons hot paprika or cayenne pepper
1 teaspoon sea salt

To serve
4 pita breads, for holding the skewer
7 ounces Greek-style yogurt
Iced purslane salad, to serve
Bulgur pilaf, to serve

Directions:
1. Roughly mince the lamb, and combine it with the hot paprika and salt. Form it into a ball, and refrigerate for approximately 3 hours.
2. Take out the meat and split it into 4 balls. Use 4 metal skewers, and form the meat around them, pressing the mixture so it forms a kebab. Put in the fridge for an additional hour.
3. Prepare your barbecue by bringing it to high heat. Place the skewers on the grill and cook them for approximately 6 minutes, making sure to flip them every minute or so.
4. Use a piece of pita bread to gently pull the skewer off the grill. Serve in a pita bread, with a side of yogurt, iced purslane salad and bulgur pilaf.

Grilled Galbi

This is a Korean recipe, and galbi means beef ribs in Korean, so this is a recipe for barbecued beef ribs with an exceptionally flavored marinade and a combination of meat and sugar.

Serves: 14

Ingredients:
3 ½ pounds beef short ribs, butterflied very thinly to one side, meat left on the bone (pyun galbi)
¾ cup sugar, divided
½ onion, roughly chopped
¼ cup Korean/nashi pear, blended (optional)
⅓-½ cup soy sauce
¼ cup cooking sake
½ teaspoon ground pepper
2 tablespoons sesame oil
3-4 cloves garlic, minced
1 teaspoon ginger, minced
2-3 green onions, sliced
Cooked rice, kimchi, or lettuce, for serving

Directions:
1. Place the ribs in a large bowl and cover them with water. Refrigerate for about half an hour. When the meat starts to pale, discard the water, leaving the ribs in the bowl.
2. Add ¼ cup of sugar and mix it with the meat. Leave it for approximately 10 minutes, and drain any liquid.
3. Use a blender to mix the onions and pear, and stir the puree with the meat. Leave it for approximately 10 minutes, and then add all the other ingredients, including the rest of the sugar. Let it stay in the fridge overnight.
4. Prepare your grill by warming it to medium-high heat. Grill the meat until it is cooked through. Serve with rice, kimchi, or lettuce.

Grilled John Dory with Salt Koji

It takes a while to prepare this meal as you need to make salt koji two weeks in advance. You can choose to use it immediately after it is made, but the right flavor will develop over a 14-day period.

Serves: 4

Ingredients:
4 John Dory fillets, approximately 1 pound

Salt koji
7 ounces dried rice koji
2 ¾ ounces good quality sea salt
13 ½ fluid ounces water

Smoky green chili moromi
1 long green chili
2 tablespoon moromi miso

Directions:
1. Mix all the ingredients for the salt koji in a bowl and combine well. Keep the koji in an airtight container at room temperature for 2 weeks. Make sure to stir it once a day.
2. Coat the fish with koji and refrigerate it for about 6 hours.
3. Preheat the barbecue to medium. Grill the chili for about 30 seconds, then take out the seeds and cut it into thin slices. Mix in the moromi.
4. Take the fish out of the marinade and pierce its skin with a skewer. You don't want any air pockets. Put 5 metal skewers through every fillet.
5. Place the fish with the skin-side down on your barbecue and grill each side for approximately 5 minutes. Remove the skewers gently and serve.

Kofta-style Kebabs

One more recipe for kebabs that come from Turkey, served with a salad on the side.

Serves: 4

Ingredients:
Koftas
1 pound lean minced lamb
4 ½ ounces trimmed lamb neck fillet, finely chopped
1 onion, finely chopped
1 clove garlic, grated
1 teaspoon ground cumin
Good pinch chili flakes (optional)
1 small bunch flat-leaf parsley, leaves and stems coarsely chopped
Sea salt and freshly ground black pepper

Salad
1 handful pickled green chilies
1 handful grated carrot
1 handful cooked white beans, such as haricot
1 small head of lettuce, trimmed and shredded
A good squeeze of lemon juice
Lemon wedges, for garnish

Directions:
1. Preheat the barbecue to medium heat.
2. Put all ingredients for the koftas in one bowl. Mix with your hands until they are nicely combined. Split the mixture into 4 balls, and then form it around metal skewers in the shape of kebabs.
3. Grill the koftas for approximately 15 minutes, flipping occasionally.
4. Divide the ingredients for the salad onto four plates. Serve the koftas with salad and a lemon wedge.

Grilled Gai Yang

Another traditional Thai chicken recipe for all of you who love Asian food.

Serves: 12

Ingredients:
1 ounce lemongrass
2 French shallots
2 teaspoons cilantro roots
2 teaspoons black peppercorns
4 garlic cloves
1 teaspoon ground turmeric, divided
1 teaspoon ground cilantro
3 teaspoon palm sugar (jaggery)
1 ½ teaspoons fish sauce
1 ½ teaspoons oyster sauce
1 ½ teaspoons Thai seasoning soy sauce
1 ½ teaspoons light soy sauce
3 tablespoons vegetable oil
1 whole chicken (about 3 pounds) butterflied

Nam jim jaew ma kham piek (tamarind jim jaew dipping sauce)
⅓ cup tamarind purée
⅓ cup palm sugar (jaggery)
3 tablespoons fish sauce
3 tablespoons boiling water
1 teaspoon chili powder
2 teaspoons roasted rice powder

Directions:
1. Use a pestle and mortar to pound the lemongrass, shallots, cilantro roots, peppercorns, garlic, turmeric, and cilantro powder. Set aside.
2. Mix the fish sauce with the palm sugar, oyster sauce, Thai seasoning soy sauce, light soy sauce, and vegetable oil. Stir well and then combine with the first mixture.
3. Coat the chicken in the marinade and leave it covered in the refrigerator for at least half an hour (up to 12 hours).

4. Prepare the dipping sauce by mixing the tamarind puree, palm sugar, fish sauce, and water in a pan. Bring it to a boil over medium heat and then cool it down. When it cools down, add the chili powder and roasted rice powder.
5. Preheat the barbecue to medium. Take the chicken out of the marinade and place on the barbecue, making sure that skin side is up. Grill, turning occasionally, until cooked through. Let it rest for 10 minutes and serve with the dipping sauce.

Traditional Malaysian Chicken Satay

Malaysians know their barbecue and definitely know their way around satay, so you should give this recipe a try.

Serves: 4

Ingredients:
½ onion, diced
½ lemongrass stem, white part only, diced
½ teaspoon curry powder
1 clove garlic, crushed
½ teaspoon fresh turmeric, diced
Pinch of paprika
2 tablespoons sugar
Salt
1 pound chicken breast, cut into 1-inch slices (you can use beef tenderloin instead)
16 bamboo skewers
1 tablespoon vegetable oil
1 cucumber, cubed

Satay sauce
1 onion, sliced
2 smashed garlic cloves
2 lemongrass stems, white part only, diced
2 dried red chilies, reconstituted in water
¼ cup peanut oil
Pinch of paprika
1 teaspoon curry powder
1 teaspoon ground turmeric
½ cup peanuts, roughly grounded
½ cup water
½ cup coconut milk
Salt
1 tablespoon sugar

Directions:
1. Prepare the satay sauce by using a pestle and mortar to pound the onion, garlic, lemongrass, and chilies.

2. Heat the peanut oil in a small pan. Add the paste and cook for a couple of minutes. Mix in the paprika, curry powder, and turmeric. Put in the peanuts, water, and coconut milk and bring it to a boil, while making sure to stir regularly. Put in the salt and sugar and simmer for an additional 20 minutes.
3. To prepare the meat, first use a blender to process the onion, lemongrass, curry powder, garlic, turmeric, and paprika. Add the salt and sugar and combine. Add cubed pieces of chicken or beef, combine, and refrigerate for a minimum of 6 hours.
4. Before grilling, place 3 pieces of meat on every skewer. Brush the meat with oil and grill for approximate 5 minutes per side. Serve with satay sauce and a side of cucumber.

Joojeh Kebap with Lemon and Pepper

This is an Iranian dish that is very simple to make. The longer you leave the chicken to marinate, the more tender it will be, so make sure to give it time.

Serves: 8

Ingredients:
2 pounds boneless skinless chicken thighs
1 onion, roughly chopped
½ cup extra virgin olive oil
1 ½ teaspoons salt
1 ½ teaspoons freshly ground black pepper
½ cup lemon juice
¾ teaspoon saffron threads
To serve: Greek yogurt, steamed rice, grilled onion, roasted tomatoes, and mint leaves

Directions:
1. Take chicken fillets and slice them into 1-inch pieces. Place them in a non-reactive bowl.
2. In a blender, mix the onion and oil and blend until it becomes smooth. Put in all the remaining ingredients and process again.
3. Pour the marinade over the chicken and coat it well. Cover with plastic wrap and put in the refrigerator overnight (or for at least 8 hours).
4. Take the chicken out of the marinade, and set the marinade aside. Thread the chicken onto skewers.
5. Brush the barbecue with oil and arrange the chicken on it. Grill for approximately 10 minutes, making sure to turn it often and baste with the reserved marinade. Do not baste in the final few minutes of cooking, so the marinade will have a chance to cook.

Korean Barbecued Brisket

This is a high-quality meat they often eat in Korea. The trick is in freezing it. You can also serve it with barbecued garlic.

Serves: 6

Ingredients:
1 ½ pounds brisket (from point or flat end)
Vegetable oil (for grilling)

Directions:
1. Put the brisket in the freezer for a minimum of 8 hours.
2. Take it out of the freezer and leave it at room temperature for approximately 2 hours.
3. Cut the brisket into slices ⅛ inch thick.
4. In the meantime, preheat your grill and oil the grates with vegetable oil. Place the brisket on the barbecue and grill each side for approximately 1 minute.

Europe's Barbecue Recipes

Barbecued Chicken with Whole Grain Orzo

This very healthy recipe for barbecued chicken originates from Greece and provides a great mix of chicken, orzo and peas.

Serves: 4-6

Ingredients:
¼ cup plain fat-free Greek yogurt, at room temperature
1 tablespoon extra-virgin olive oil, divided
1 large clove garlic, minced
Juice and zest of 1 lemon
Salt and freshly ground black pepper
3 boneless skinless chicken thighs
1 cup whole wheat or other whole grain orzo
1 cup frozen petite peas, thawed and patted dry
4 tablespoons chopped fresh herbs, such as basil and tarragon
2 ounces finely crumbled goat cheese, at room temperature

Directions:
1. In a medium bowl, combine the yogurt, 2 teaspoons of oil, garlic, ½ teaspoon of salt, ½ teaspoon of pepper, and lemon juice. Mix until they are well blended.
2. Prepare your outdoor grill to medium. Use the remaining teaspoon of oil to rub the chicken thighs and sprinkle them with 1/4 teaspoon of salt and 1/2 teaspoon of pepper. Grill for about 10 minutes on each side, until the meat has nice grill marks. Move them to a cutting board and let it cool for a minimum of 5 minutes.
3. Boil a pot of water and put in the orzo, and cook according to the directions on the package. Mix in the peas in the last minute of cooking. Drain the water, reserving 1 cup.
4. Mix the orzo and peas with the yogurt mixture, and add 3 tablespoons of fresh herbs, the goat cheese, and the reserved cooking liquid. Mix until well combined and move to a plate.

5. Cut the chicken into thin slices and put it over the orzo. Sprinkle lemon zest and the remaining tablespoon of fresh herbs. Serve.

Barbecued Lamb Chops

Try these beautiful barbecued lamb chops the way they're prepared in Italy.

Serves: 6

Ingredients:
⅓ tablespoon garlic, crushed
1 tablespoon fresh rosemary leaves
1 teaspoon fresh thyme leaves
Pinch cayenne pepper
Coarse sea salt
⅛ cup extra-virgin olive oil
6 lamb chops, about 1 inch thick

Directions:
1. Put the garlic, rosemary, thyme, cayenne, and salt in a food processor. Blend it until it is nicely mixed. Add the olive oil and process again until it makes a paste.
2. Use the paste to brush lamb chops on both sides. Refrigerate for at least 1 hour.
3. When you take the lamb chops out of your refrigerator, let them come to room temperature, which should take no more than 25 minutes.
4. Preheat your barbecue to high heat. Place the chops on the grates and grill for 2 minutes before flipping them. Grill for an additional three minutes until they are of medium doneness.

Barbecued Chicken with Parmesan and Spinach

Exotic Italian mix of grilled chicken and spinach, combined with Parmesan cheese

Serves: 2-4

Ingredients:
2 boneless chicken breasts
4 tablespoons baby spinach leaves
2 tablespoons pine nuts, toasted
2 tablespoons fresh lemon juice
1-2 teaspoons grated lemon zest
⅓ cup plus 2 teaspoons olive oil
Salt and freshly ground black pepper
2 tablespoons Parmesan, freshly grated

Directions:
1. Preheat your grill to medium-high heat and oil the grates. Season the chicken with salt and pepper. Grill each side for approximately 5 minutes, until it is cooked through.
2. Mix the spinach, pine nuts, lemon juice, and lemon peel in a food blender. Process, and while it is running, slowly add ⅓ cup of the oil. Process until you get a creamy composition. Put in the salt and process once again. You can transfer part of the pesto to the freezer and store it for future use.
3. Move the rest of the pesto to a bowl and mix with the Parmesan cheese. Season with salt and pepper to your liking. Sprinkle the pesto over the chicken.

Grilled Spanish Potatoes

This is a traditional Spanish recipe which can be great as a side, or even as a starter.

Serves: 4-8

Ingredients:
5 large red or yellow potatoes, scrubbed
2 tablespoons salt, plus more for seasoning
2 plum tomatoes
4 tablespoons olive oil
Freshly ground black pepper
3 cloves garlic, chopped
1 cup prepared mayonnaise
2 teaspoons Spanish paprika
2 teaspoons pureed chipotle chilies in adobo
2 tablespoons finely chopped fresh flat-leaf parsley

Directions:
1. Place the potatoes in a big pot of cold water and add 2 tablespoons of salt. Cook for approximately 12 to 15 minutes, drain, and let it cool down. Cut it into pieces that should be around 1 inch thick.
2. Preheat your barbecue to high heat. Use the oil to brush the tomatoes and season to your taste with salt and pepper. Grill them for approximately ten minutes, until they become soft. When charred, take them off the barbecue.
3. Put the tomatoes, garlic, mayonnaise, paprika, and chipotle in a blender or food processor. Process until smooth, seasoning with salt and pepper.
4. Brush the potato slices with oil, put them on the barbecue, and grill for approximately 2 minutes on each side. Move them to a serving plate and sprinkle with the parsley. Serve with a side of chipotle sauce.

Barbecued Mediterranean Fish

When you are in the mood for a family barbecue, fish is a good way to go and Branzino with this Mediterranean marinade is an excellent choice.

Serves: 2

Ingredients:
2 whole fish such as Orata, or Branzino, scaled and gutted
Olive oil
Sea salt and freshly ground pepper
1 large orange, cut into thin slices
1 bunch parsley
1 bunch tarragon

For the sherry vinaigrette
¼ cup aged sherry vinegar
1 small shallot, chopped
2 teaspoons Dijon mustard
Salt and freshly ground pepper
3 tablespoons chopped fresh tarragon
½ cup Spanish olive oil

Directions:
1. Prepare your grill to medium-high heat. Coat the fish with olive oil and use salt and pepper to your liking. Stuff the cavities of the fish with slices of orange, parsley and tarragon.
2. To make the vinaigrette, mix the vinegar, shallot, mustard, and mustard in a blender. Season with salt and pepper, and process until it becomes smooth and then gradually add the oil.
3. Place the fish on the grates and cook it for about 6 minutes per side. Transfer it to a serving plate and sprinkle immediately with the vinaigrette.

Chicken Breasts with Parsley and Mint Sauce

Another traditional Spanish recipe which combines chicken rubbed in spices with an attractive mint-parsley sauce.

Serves: 4

Ingredients:
For the spice rubbed chicken
1 tablespoon Spanish paprika
1 tablespoon smoked paprika
2 teaspoons ground cumin seeds
2 teaspoons ground mustard seeds
2 teaspoons ground fennel seeds
1 teaspoon coarsely ground black pepper
2 teaspoons sea salt
4 8-ounce boneless chicken breasts
Olive oil

Mint-Parsley Sauce
12 ounces fresh mint leaves
6 ounces fresh flat-leaf parsley
6 garlic cloves, sliced
2 serrano chilies, sliced and grilled
2 tablespoons Dijon mustard
2 tablespoons honey
¾ cup olive oil
Salt and freshly ground black pepper
Water

Directions:
1. Preheat your barbecue to high heat.
2. Prepare the mint-parsley sauce by putting the mint, parsley, garlic, and serrano chilis in a food blender and processing until it is smooth. Put in the mustard and honey and blend again until nicely combined. Gradually add the olive oil while the processor is still running.

Move it to a bowl and add a tablespoon of cold water (or more) to thin the consistency. Season with salt and pepper to your liking.
3. In a little bowl, mix the paprika, cumin, mustard, fennel, pepper, and salt.
4. Use a couple of teaspoons of oil to rub the chicken breasts on the skin side. Place them on the grill with the rubbed side down. Grill for approximately 5 minutes, flip, and then grill for additional 5 minutes.
5. Move the chicken to a plate and drizzle with mint-parsley sauce. Let it absorb the flavor for about 5 minutes. You can serve the extra sauce on the side.

Lamb Chops with Garlic Salsa

This is a traditional English recipe that offers various herbs to add to the salsa taste.

Serves: 4

Ingredients:
4 lamb chops, shoulder, thin
8 stalks purple sprouting broccoli, cut in half lengthways
8 spears trimmed asparagus
8 garlic flowers

Wild garlic salsa verde
Large handful wild garlic leaves
Small handful Vietnamese mint, roughly sliced
Small handful basil leaves, roughly sliced
Small handful parsley leaves, roughly sliced
Small handful mint leaves, roughly sliced
2 red birds eye chilies, cut
4 anchovy fillets in olive oil
1 teaspoon malt vinegar
2 tablespoon fish sauce
1 teaspoon Dijon mustard
1 teaspoon lemon zest
Pinch of salt and pepper
¼ cup olive oil

Directions:
1. Prepare the salsa verde by using a mortar and pestle to pound the herbs, wild garlic leaves, and chilies. Put in the anchovies and 1 tablespoon of anchovy oil, vinegar, fish sauce, mustard, lemon zest, salt, pepper, and olive oil. Mix well.
2. Coat the lamb chops with salsa verde.
3. Grill for approximately 3 minutes per side, basting with additional salsa verde when flipping. Once you flip the meat, add asparagus and broccoli to the grill and cook them until they are lightly charred.

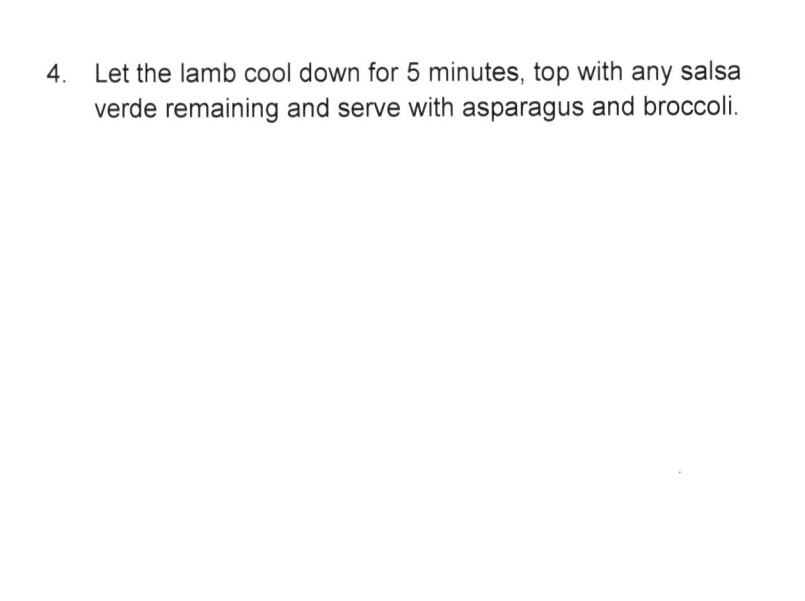

4. Let the lamb cool down for 5 minutes, top with any salsa verde remaining and serve with asparagus and broccoli.

Greek-style Barbecued Seafood

Seafood is a traditional part of Greek cuisine and this seafood recipe shows just how great a combination of flavored seafood can taste.

Serves: 6-8

Ingredients:
3 cloves garlic, finely chopped
1 tablespoon oregano leaves, roughly chopped
2 tablespoons lemon juice, plus lemon halves, to serve
½ cup olive oil, divided
2 (18-ounce) octopuses, cleaned, cut into large pieces
7 ounces cuttlefish, cleaned, cut into large pieces
18 ounces extra-large green prawns
18 ounces mussels, scrubbed, bearded
½ cup dry white wine
Salt and black pepper

Directions:
1. In a bowl, place the fresh garlic, oregano, lemon juice and ¼ cup of olive oil. Season with salt and pepper, to your liking and mix.
2. Combine the octopus, cuttlefish, and prawns in a large bowl. Over it, drizzle the remaining ¼ cup of olive oil and mix to coat them well.
3. Preheat your barbecue to high heat and cook octopus and cuttlefish for 4 minutes on each side, or until tender, and the prawns for 2 minutes on each side, or until just cooked.
4. In the meantime, place the prepared mussels and white wine in a saucepan over high heat. Cover them and cook for 4 minutes, or until the shells open up. Discard any that do not open.
5. Drain the mussels and transfer them to a plate with the grilled seafood. Drizzle the sauce over, and serve with lemon.

Barbecued Chicken from Tuscany

Italians have thought of this extremely easy way to grill your chicken. The marinade will give it great flavor and rocket salad mix and lemon are there to improve its taste even more.

Serves: 8

Ingredients:
2 small handfuls chopped rosemary
½ cup olive oil, plus more for grilling
Juice of 2 lemons
Salt and pepper
2 whole chickens
3 large handfuls rocket salad mix
Lemon, to serve
Special equipment: 2 foil-covered bricks

Directions:
1. Preheat your barbecue to medium-high heat.
2. In a resealable plastic bag, put the chopped rosemary, olive oil, and lemon juice. Season with salt and pepper.
3. Remove the backbone from the chicken and place the chicken into the bag with the marinade. Seal the bag and let it marinade for at least an hour.
4. Oil the grates of your barbecue. Take the chicken out of the marinade and put it on the grill, skin side down. Grill until both sides are cooked. Put 2 bricks wrapped in foil on the chicken to weigh it down. Let it rest for 5 minutes once it is grilled.

Spanish Shrimps with Garlic and Thyme

This traditional Spanish recipe will be welcomed by all the shrimp lovers out there.

Serves: 4-6

Ingredients:
¾ cup olive oil, divided
3 tablespoons freshly chopped thyme leaves, divided
1 ½ tablespoons ancho chili powder
6 cloves garlic, coarsely chopped
24 large shrimp, shelled and deveined
Salt and freshly ground black pepper
3 cloves garlic, thinly sliced
1 sprig of oregano, for garnish
Special equipment: wooden skewers soaked in water

Directions:
1. Prepare your barbecue by heating it to medium.
2. Mix ¼ cup of olive oil, 2 tablespoons of the thyme, ancho chili powder, and chopped garlic to prepare the marinade. Brush the shrimps with the mixture and put them on skewers.
3. Pour the remaining oil in a small pan, together with the sliced garlic. Cook thoroughly, and then remove the garlic pieces to a platter. Save the oil.
4. Turn the heat of your barbecue up to high. Take the shrimps out of the marinade and season them with salt and pepper to your liking. Grill them for about 2 minutes on each side.
5. Remove the shrimp from skewers and place it on a plate. Drizzle with the reserved oil and the garlic chips. Garnish with a spring of oregano and the remaining thyme.

Greek Rolled Minced Lamb with Tzatziki

They are extremely easy to make and can feed a big crowd, so they are ideal for big barbecues.

Serves: 4

Ingredients:
1 pound ground lamb
2 cloves garlic, crushed and minced
1 tablespoon olive oil
1 tablespoon water
1 ½ teaspoons sweet paprika
½ teaspoon hot paprika
Salt and freshly ground pepper
Olive oil

Tzatziki
1 small English cucumber
4 cloves garlic
2 cups Greek-style yogurt
5 ounces quark cheese
1 teaspoon olive oil
Salt and freshly ground pepper

Directions:
1. Begin to prepare the tzatziki by washing and peeling the cucumber. Grate it, and place it in a bowl and squeeze the juice out of it. Press the peeled garlic in another bowl. Add the yogurt, quark, and olive oil. Mix until creamy, and then combine it with the cucumber. Season it to taste with salt and pepper and keep it in the fridge.
2. Preheat the barbecue to medium, and oil the grates.
3. Place the minced lamb in a dish. Mix in the garlic, and put in 1 tablespoon of olive oil and 1 tablespoon of water, as well as the paprika, salt, and pepper. Combine well. Moisten your hands and make 16 little rolls. Press the rolls into strips about 3 inches in length. Shape them around skewers and place on the grill, flipping frequently.
4. Serve with tzatziki for dipping.

Barbecued Chicken with Piri-Piri Sauce

Portuguese people wanted no one to resist this chicken, which is why they made a marinade that consists of white wine, olive oil, and brandy.

Serves: 12-16

Ingredients:
1 whole chicken (3-4 pounds), butterflied

Marinade
1 ½ lemons, juiced
½ lemon, sliced
7 cloves garlic, roughly chopped
6 fresh bay leaves, roughly chopped
1 tablespoon sweet paprika
2 tablespoons sea salt
1 cup beer
1 cup dry white wine
2 tablespoons whisky or brandy
2 tablespoons extra-virgin olive oil

Piri-piri sauce
4 cloves garlic
2 French shallots
1 lemon, juiced
10 medium red chilies, whole
¾-inch piece fresh ginger
1 tablespoon red wine vinegar
⅓ cup extra-virgin olive oil
2 teaspoon sea salt
1 teaspoon sweet paprika

Rice pilaf
2 tablespoons olive oil
½ onion, finely chopped
1 clove garlic, crushed
1 cup long-grain white rice
1 ½ cups hot chicken stock

a handful of parsley sprigs

Directions:
1. Set aside the lemon slices, and prepare the marinade by mixing all the other ingredients together.
2. Use a sharp knife to make slits all over the chicken. Place the chicken in a deep dish and let the marinade penetrate into the meat. Massage it into the meat.
3. Arrange the lemon slices on top, cover it, and leave in the refrigerator overnight.
4. Prepare the coals under the spit until they glow, or heat the barbecue to medium-high. Remove the chicken from the marinade, and discard any bay leaves and garlic left on it, but keep the marinade. Put the chicken in a barbecue cage and firmly close the clamp. Cook for about 45 minutes, turning and basting with the kept marinade occasionally. Do not baste in the final few minutes of cooking, so the marinade will cook.
5. Prepare the Piri-Piri sauce by combining the ingredients in a blender and processing until smooth. Transfer into a clay pot and cook for 10 minutes over the coals, stirring constantly.
6. To prepare the rice pilaf, heat a terracotta pot over the coals and put in the olive oil. Sauté the garlic and onion and then put in the rice. Toast it shortly until coated with oil and beginning to brown. Add the parsley and hot stock. Cover with a lid and transfer the pot off the direct heat. Cook for an additional 12 minutes until the rice becomes tender. Leave it to rest and absorb all the liquid.
7. When the chicken is nearly done, brush it with Piri-Piri sauce. Cook for an additional minute.

Cypriot Sheftalia

You don't have to go all the way to Cyprus to try this great homemade sausage recipe. You can serve them with oiled and barbecued pita bread.

Serves: 8-10

Ingredients:
2 ¼ pounds coarsely ground pork leg or neck mince
4-5 red onions, coarsely chopped
4-5 small bunches parsley, coarsely chopped
1 tablespoon salt, or to taste
1 tablespoon cracked black pepper, or to taste
Washed caul fat

Directions:
1. Mix the pork, onion, and parsley in a bowl. Use your hands to combine the ingredients and season to taste with salt and pepper.
2. Put the caul fat on a cutting board. Take a big piece of the mixture and make an oval form. Put in on the corner of the caul. Roll with your fingers to coat the mince mixture. Using kitchen shears, cut the fat to size and repeat the process for all the mixture.
3. Place the sausages on a hot grill. Season them with salt to your taste and cook for approximately 12 minutes. When they are cooked through, remove and serve.

Africa's Barbecue Recipes

Smoked Chicken Wings with Mint, Dates and Chilies

Careful mixture of spices and herbs they've created in Morocco will give your chicken wings an absolutely amazing taste

Serves: 20

Ingredients:
For the marinade
¼ cup salt
1 tablespoon honey
4 cloves garlic, peeled and crushed
5 pounds chicken wings separated at the joint, tips discarded

For the quick pickled chilies and dates
½ cup rice wine vinegar
¼ cup sugar
1 tablespoon soy sauce
10 Medjool dates, pits removed and finely diced
4-5 spring onions, finely cut on the bias
1 fresno chili, halved lengthwise and finely sliced
Sunflower oil, for grilling
Salt and black pepper
3 tablespoons smoked paprika
2 tablespoons toasted sesame oil
¼ cup fresh cilantro leaves, chopped
¼ cup fresh mint leaves, chopped

Directions:
1. In a big bowl, combine 6 cups of water, salt, honey, and garlic. Whisk until the salt dissolves and put in the wings. Turn to coat. Cover with plastic wrap and refrigerate for approximately 2 hours.

2. In the meantime, prepare the other mixture in another big bowl. Mix the rice wine vinegar, sugar, and soy sauce. Whisk until blended and then put in the dates, spring onions, and chili.
3. Take the chicken out of the marinade and drain it well.
4. Prepare your grill, making sure there is an indirect heat zone. Brush the grates with oil.
5. Season the wings to your liking with salt and pepper and toss with smoked paprika and sesame oil. Grill for about 7 minutes per side, until the skin of the wings gets crispy. Transfer them to the indirect heat, and let them cook through for about 12 minutes.
6. Transfer the wings to a big bowl. Put the chopped herbs into the picked date mixture, whisk, and then combine with the wings. Coat the wings evenly before serving.

Grilled Lamb Sosatie

Sosatie is a term used for skewers in South Africa, and this marinated lamb recipe is ideal for a nice afternoon barbecue.

Serves: 12

Ingredients:
12 wooden skewers
5 ½ pounds lamb cut into 1-inch pieces
¼ cup coriander (seeds)
1 ½ tablespoons salt
2 teaspoons ground ginger
2 teaspoons ground black pepper
½ teaspoon chili flakes
¼ cup olive oil
1 tablespoon brown sugar
1 tablespoon curry powder
3 cups white vinegar
2 cups malt vinegar
36 dried apricots
36 bay leaves

Directions:
1. Soak skewers in water for about half an hour.
2. Put the lamb into a bowl and sprinkle with the coriander, salt, ginger, pepper, and chili flakes. Use your hands to blend the spices with the meat.
3. In a pan, heat the oil to medium. Stir in the brown sugar, curry powder, and vinegar and bring it to a boil. You can pour the liquid over the meat while it is hot, but it is better if you have time to let it cool down. Add the bay leaves and apricots and refrigerate for at least 2 hours.
4. Thread the lamb, folded bay leaves and apricots on the skewers. Reserve the marinade.

5. Heat the barbecue to medium-high. Grill the skewers on each of the four sides for approximately 2 minutes. During cooking, brush with the reserved marinade. Do not remove from the heat until the final application of marinade has time to cook.

Moroccan-Style Lamb Kebabs

Moroccans know their way around spices and they definitely showcase that with this marinated lamb recipe.

Serves: 14

Ingredients:
3 ½ pounds boneless skinless lamb fillets, thinly sliced
1 teaspoon ground ginger
4 cloves garlic, peeled and crushed
1 teaspoon paprika
1 heaping teaspoon cumin seeds, coarsely crushed and toasted
½ teaspoon ground cinnamon
1 handful fresh parsley, roughly chopped
1 handful fresh mint, roughly chopped
1 handful fresh cilantro, roughly chopped
Salt
Freshly ground black pepper
Runny honey

Directions:
1. Put the lamb in a glass bowl. Mix in all the ingredients except the salt, pepper, and honey. Stir to coat well. Marinate for about half an hour.
2. Thread the lamb pieces on skewers and season to your liking with salt and pepper.
3. Grill the skewers until they are well cooked. Season them with honey just before serving.

Grilled Mechoui with Yogurt and Mint

An excellent and downright easy recipe for grilled lamb, which combined with cooled minted yogurt, provides an exquisite taste.

Serves: 10

Ingredients:
2 ½ pounds lamb backstraps or fillets, cut into long strips about 1 inch wide
1 tablespoon ground cumin
1 tablespoon sweet paprika
2 tablespoons chopped garlic
1 tablespoon chopped cilantro
1 tablespoon chopped flat-leaf parsley
1 tablespoon lemon juice
A generous drizzle of olive oil
Salt

Minted yogurt
1 cup natural yogurt
¼ teaspoon sugar
3 teaspoon chopped mint

Directions:
1. In a big bowl, combine the lamb with all the other ingredients. Make sure to cover the lamb nicely in the marinade. Cover with plastic wrap and put it in the refrigerator for about an hour.
2. Mix the ingredients for minted yogurt in a food processor and keep it cool in your refrigerator.
3. Preheat your barbecue to medium-high heat. Grill the lamb until it is medium-rare. Serve alongside the yogurt.

Traditional South African Braai

Beer is the secret ingredient that gives this recipe the traditional South African braai flavor, and with the mix of tuna and pork, everyone will find something they like.

Serves: 6-8:

Ingredients:
1 cup sweet soy sauce (ketjap manis)
1 cup sticky dark brown sugar
⅓ cup olive oil
½ cup ginger, peeled and roughly sliced
10 cloves garlic, peeled
3 tablespoons tomato paste
2 cups warm water
Juice and grated rind of 1 lemon
4 tablespoons fresh thyme, stems removed
2 whole red birds eye chilies; slightly split
6 tuna steaks
6 pork chops
Large handful of fresh sage leaves
1 bottle lager

Directions:
1. Put the soy sauce, brown sugar, olive oil, ginger, garlic, and tomato paste in a food processor. Process it until it becomes smooth, then add the water before mixing it again. Once it is nicely combined, transfer it to a frying pan and bring it to a simmer. Put in the lemon zest and juice, thyme and chilies, and let it simmer for an additional 5 minutes. Let it cool and when it cools down, move it to a jug.
2. Place the tuna in one large re-sealable bag, and the pork in another. Divide the marinade between the bags. Put the sage leaves in with the pork chops and turn to coat. Put both bags in the refrigerator.
3. Prepare your grill and cook the pork chops first. Grill them for approximately 4 minutes on each side and, in order to get the original South African flavor, sprinkle it with beer during cooking.

4. As for the tuna steaks, place them on the grill, too, and grill them for approximately 1 minute on each side.

Grilled Eggplants with Warm Grilled Bread

If you are preparing a barbecue and want to surprise your vegan friends with a fresh, new recipe, be sure to try this recipe from South Africa. They will be thrilled.

Serves: 4-6

Ingredients:
For the cumin and eggplant dip
2 medium-sized eggplants, trimmed and sliced thick on the vertical
2 teaspoons cumin
1-2 cloves garlic
1 ½ cups yogurt
Juice and zest of half a lemon
Salt and coarsely ground pepper to taste

For the roosterkoek bread
14 ounces plain flour, plus extra for dusting
1 packet dried yeast
1 teaspoon salt
2 teaspoons caster sugar
¼ cup vegetable oil
1 cup warm water

Directions:
1. Cook the eggplants on the grill for about 30 minutes, making sure to flip them occasionally.
2. Put the cumin in a pan on the grill and toast it.
3. Chop the eggplants and garlic. Mix them with toasted cumin and add the yogurt, lemon juice and zest. Season with salt and pepper to your liking.
4. Mix the yeast, ½ cup of warm water, and sugar. Leave it to sit until it starts to foam. In another bowl, whisk the flour and salt. Add the yeast mix, as well as the oil, and enough water to make the dough a bit moist.
5. Put some flour on a surface and transfer the dough to it. Knead for approximately 5 minutes before placing it into an oiled bowl. Cover it with a damp cloth and leave it for an hour to rise.

6. Split the mixture into about 12 pieces and shape them into flattened balls. Put them onto a lightly greased tray and cover with damp cloth. Leave it for additional 15 minutes to rise.
7. Place the dough balls on the barbecue and grill until they become puffed up and crusty on the outside, turning a couple of times. Serve immediately with the eggplant mixture.

Peanut Chicken Skewers with Yogurt

This recipe is known in Sierra Leone and is often a part of various celebrations.

Serves: 10

Ingredients:
2 tablespoons vegetable oil
1 onion, finely chopped
2 garlic cloves, finely chopped
½ long red chili, finely chopped
1 tablespoon tomato paste
2 tablespoons crunchy peanut butter
½ cup water
½ cup coconut cream
2 teaspoons brown sugar
1 lemon, juiced
2 ½ pounds boneless skinless chicken thighs
Cilantro sprigs and lemon wedges, to serve

Ginger yogurt
1 cup thick Greek-style yogurt
3 teaspoons grated ginger
1 garlic clove, crushed
1 lemon, juiced

Directions:
1. Heat 1 tablespoon of oil in a pan over medium heat. Put in the onion and cook for approximately 3 minutes, stirring constantly. Add the garlic, chili, and tomato paste and cook for an additional minute. Put in the peanut butter, ½ cup of water, and coconut cream. Simmer until it begins to thicken and then add the sugar and lemon juice. Season to your liking and leave it to cool down.
2. Slice the chicken into pieces 1-inch-thick and put them in a big bowl. Once the marinade is cooled down, pour it over the chicken and stir to coat. Put it in the fridge for about 3 hours.

3. Prepare the ginger yogurt by combining all ingredients in one bowl. Season to taste with salt and pepper and place it in the refrigerator.
4. Put the chicken onto skewers. Brush the grates of your barbecue with a tablespoon of oil. Season the chicken skewers according to your taste and grill them for approximately 8 minutes, making sure that both sides are cooked.
5. Let the skewers cool down for about 5 minutes, sprinkle with ginger yogurt, and serve with lemon wedges and cilantro.

Whole Brined Fish with Ujeni Ndiwo and Nsima

This recipe comes from Malawi, an African country where the tradition is to eat with your bare hands.

Serves: 6

Ingredients:
For the fish
1 whole fish, about 1 ½ pounds, such as a snapper
1 tablespoon olive oil
2 tablespoons chili sauce
Juice of ½ a lemon
1 red chili, finely chopped
A small bunch of cilantro, torn

Nsima
1 ½ cups maize flour
4 cups vegetable stock
Salt and pepper
2 tablespoons butter

Ujeni ndiwo
1 small onion, sliced
1 tablespoon olive oil
1 small bunch ginger
2 cups greens (cabbage, spinach, bean leaves, kale, mustard leaves)
½ cup water
1 tomato, sliced
Salt

Directions:
1. Put the fish in a deep, oval dish and pour the olive oil, chili sauce, and lemon juice over it. Massage the marinade into the fish and put it into the refrigerator for 1-2 hours.
2. About half an hour before grilling the fish, put 4 cups of vegetable stock in a pan and heat. Gradually sprinkle in the maize flour in ½ cup batches. Whisk constantly to keep from creating lumps. Whisk until you get a porridge-like texture. Add the butter, stir, and cover.
3. Take the fish out of the fridge, put on a piece of tin foil and pour the marinade remaining in the dish over the fish. Wrap it so the marinade stays on the foil and doesn't drip.
4. Place the foil on the barbecue and grill for approximately 8 minutes per side.
5. In the meantime, put onions, oil and ginger in a pan and cook until they become softened. Put in the greens and then add the water, stirring until it is completely absorbed. Stir in the chopped tomato and season to your liking with salt.
6. Move the fish to a serving dish once it is done with cooking and garnish with fresh chili and chopped cilantro. Serve with the nsima.

Hanger Steak with Basting Mix and Biryani Spices

Hanger actually translates as the butcher's steak. You should cook it to medium-rare to keep all the juices.

Serves: 2

Ingredients:
9 ounces onglet/hanger steak
Sea salt
Sheba

Biryani spices
1 tablespoon cardamom pods
1 tablespoon star anise
1 tablespoon dehydrated grapefruit, orange, and lemon zest
1 tablespoon coriander
1 tablespoon Madras curry powder
1 tablespoon roasted chili powder
1 tablespoon dehydrated tomato powder
1 tablespoon freeze-dried mandarin powder
1 tablespoon French shallots, sliced and pan-fried

Basting mix
½ cup soy sauce
Pinch of sugar
2 red chilies, finely chopped
2 garlic cloves, crushed

Directions:
1. Prepare the biryani spices by using pestle and mortar to crush the cardamom pods and star anise. Put in the dehydrated citrus zest and the coriander, and continue pounding. Next, put in the curry powder, roasted chili powder, and tomato powder and pound again. Finally, put in the mandarin powder, pound one more time and add the shallots.

2. Trim all the sinews and extra fat from the steak. Coat it thoroughly in the biryani spices and season liberally with salt. Leave the steak at room temperature for approximately 3 hours to marinate.
3. Prepare the basting mix by combining the soy sauce, sugar, chilies, and garlic in a little bowl.
4. Baste the steak and place it on the barbecue. Grill for approximately 7 minutes. Allow it to cool down for 5 minutes prior to serving with sheba.

Spicy Shish Kebab with Pepper

If you are a fan of spicy food, the good news is – people in Morocco are, too! This is why they came up with this kebab recipe for you to try.

Serves: 16

Ingredients:
4 pounds beef chuck roast
1 teaspoon meat tenderizer (salt free)
2 tablespoons seasoned salt
½ teaspoon ground black pepper
2 hot peppers, finely chopped
2 large sweet onions
2 bell peppers
1 teaspoon salt
2 tablespoons cooking oil
1 tablespoon peanut butter
1 bottle beer (optional)

Directions:
1. Slice your meat into chunks of 1-inch thickness. Put in meat tenderizer, seasoned salt and black pepper. Combine well. Put in chopped hot pepper and leave it for 20 minutes for the seasonings to set.
2. In the meantime, slice onions and bell peppers into 1-inch pieces.
3. Once the meat is seasoned, add the oil and mix. Put in the peanut butter and coat the meat evenly.
4. Thread the meat, sweet pepper and onions on the skewers.
5. Grill the skewers until they are cooked, flipping them and splashing beer on them occasionally for flavor.

Oceania's Barbecue Recipes

Barbecued Swordfish

Swordfish is a famous specialty in Indonesia and with this recipe, you can bring that specialty to your outdoor barbecue.

Serves: 6

Ingredients:
⅓ cup soy sauce
¼ cup canola or peanut oil, plus extra for brushing on the grill
2 teaspoons grated lemon zest (2 lemons)
¼ cup freshly squeezed lemon juice
¼ cup minced or finely chopped ginger root
2 tablespoons minced garlic (4 cloves)
2 tablespoons Dijon mustard
6 (8-ounce, 1-inch thick) swordfish steaks
Sea salt

Directions:
1. In a bowl, combine the soy sauce, canola oil, lemon zest, lemon juice, ginger root, garlic, and mustard.
2. Transfer half of the sauce to a flat plate just big enough to hold the swordfish pieces in one layer. Put the fish over the sauce and sprinkle the remaining half of the sauce over it. Use plastic wrap to cover it and put it into the refrigerator for a minimum of 4 hours, preferably overnight.
3. Prepare your grill to medium-high heat, and brush the grates with oil so your fish doesn't stick to them.
4. Take the swordfish out of the marinade and throw away the marinade. Season the fish with salt.
5. Grill each side for about 5 minutes, until it loses its pink color in the middle. Put it on a plate, cover with aluminum foil and let it cool down for 10 minutes before serving.

Quickly Fried Squid with Garlic

This simple Australian recipe is great if you wish to see how squid tastes.

Serves: 10

Ingredients:
2 ½ pounds fresh squid, cleaned and cut into rounds or strips
2-3 garlic cloves, sliced
2-3 red chillies, sliced
Olive oil

Directions:
1. Preheat your grill to high. Oil the grates, and then place the squid, along with the garlic and chilies, on the grill. Keep moving and turning the squid frequently, as it cooks very quickly.
2. Season with salt to your liking. Serve while it's hot.

Filipino-style Pork Skewers

If you are in the mood for pork skewers, why don't you try it the Filipino way? This simple recipe is ideal for summer barbecues, and you can choose between the beer and lemonade for the marinade depending on what kind of party it is.

Serves: 10

Ingredients:
2 ½ pounds pork belly
1 cup soy sauce
1 head garlic, peeled and minced
1 onion, finely chopped
¼ cup Calamansi juice or lemon juice
1 teaspoon ground black pepper
¼ cup brown or white sugar
½ cup banana or tomato ketchup
½ cup lemonade or beer (optional)
20 bamboo skewers, soaked in water for 30 minutes

Directions:
1. Slice the pork into long thin pieces, about 2 inches wide and a ¼-inch thick.
2. In a big bowl, combine the pork with the soy sauce, garlic, onion, Calamansi juice, pepper, sugar, banana ketchup, and lemonade (or beer). Put it in the refrigerator for about half an hour, flipping it from time to time.
3. Put the pork on soaked skewers. Keep the marinade.
4. Preheat your grill to medium-high. Flip the skewers and brush with the reserved marinade occasionally. Do not baste in the final minutes of cooking, to allow the marinade to cook.

Grilled Avocado with Mint and Black Pepper

This is an excellent starter or a salad when you are preparing your barbecue. The trick is to use slightly firm avocados.

Serves: 4

Ingredients:
4 firm but ripe avocados
7 ounces labneh (or cream cheese)
Juice of 1 lemon, divided
2 tablespoons extra-virgin olive oil, divided
¼ cup dill
¼ cup basil
¼ cup cilantro leaves and a little soft stem from the top leaves
¼ cup mint
Salt
Freshly cracked black pepper

Directions:
1. Cut all the avocados in half. Leave the skin on, but take out the stones. Cut the halves again into halves or even thirds.
2. Put the labneh in a bowl, then put in half of the lemon juice and half of the oil. Mix it a bit to loosen the cheese, but you don't have to entirely combine the mixture.
3. Chop the herbs and mix half into the cheese.
4. Grill the avocado, placing them with the cut side down. Once cooked, flip carefully and grill the other side. Move to a serving plate and remove the skin.
5. Put the labneh mixture onto the avocado. Sprinkle the other half of herbs, and mix the remaining lemon juice and olive oil to dress the salad. Season with salt and pepper.

Australian Steak with Grilled Corn Cobs

This is how Australians prepare their steaks. A simple recipe, but exquisite taste thanks to a great salsa combination.

Serves: 4

Ingredients:
2 medium tomatoes, diced
1 small red onion, finely chopped
1 red pepper, diced
¼ cup cilantro leaves
1 clove garlic, crushed
2 tablespoons olive oil
4 6-ounce blade steaks
Grilled corn cobs, to serve

Directions
1. Prepare your barbecue by bringing it to medium-high heat.
2. Mix the tomato, onion, pepper, cilantro, garlic, and olive oil. Season it with salt and pepper.
3. Grill the steak for approximately 3 minutes per side, until medium-rare. Move them to a cutting board and let them cool down for a couple of minutes. Slice diagonally and serve them with salsa and grilled corn cobs.

Baby Pork Ribs with Rosemary and Vincotto

The cooking process is easy and you can easily feed the crowd at your barbecue with this great Australian recipe everyone will love

Serves: 18

Ingredients:
4 ½ pounds American-style baby pork ribs
2 tablespoons olive oil
4 garlic cloves, finely chopped
2 red onions, finely chopped
1 tablespoon finely chopped rosemary
⅓ cup vincotto
2 tablespoons brown sugar
2 tablespoons tomato ketchup

Directions:
1. Put the ribs into a deep roasting pan. Cover them with boiling water, cover with foil, and bake for an hour at 320°F. Dry the ribs and refrigerate them once they are cooled down.
2. Prepare the agrodolce glaze by heating the olive oil in a pan and adding the garlic and onion. Fry over medium-low heat for approximately 10 minutes, while stirring, then add the rosemary and cook for an additional minute. Finally, put in the vincotto, brown sugar, and ketchup. increase heat to high and bring to a quick boil. Reduce heat to low and let simmer for about 2 minutes.
3. Heat your barbecue to medium. Coat the ribs in the agrodolce glaze. Grill them for about 20 minutes, turning them often.

Pork Ribs with Orange Marinade

Due to the fact that the marinade needs to stay on overnight, this recipe takes a bit of your time, but it will be worth it when you try the delightful taste of these Australian pork ribs.

Serves: 10

Ingredients:
2 ½ pounds pork spare ribs
Celery salad, radish, rocket mix

Orange marinade
2 tablespoons maple syrup
⅓ cup teriyaki sauce
Grated rind of ½ an orange
Juice of 1 orange juice
1 tablespoon grated ginger
4 green onions, sliced
1 tablespoon rice bran oil

Directions:
1. Prepare orange marinade by mixing all the ingredients in a shallow platter. Put in the pork ribs and make sure they are nicely coated. Cover with plastic wrap and put them in the refrigerator for the night. When you take them out of the fridge, leave the platter for half an hour at room temperature before grilling.
2. Prepare your grill by warming it to medium heat. Take the ribs out of the marinade and grill for about 30 minutes, making sure to baste with the marinade occasionally and turn often. Ensure that your final application of marinade has time to cook before removing the ribs from the heat.
3. Cut the ribs between short bones. Use radish, rocket mix, and celery as a salad.

Chicken Wings with Grilled Corn Cobs

You have to love barbecued chicken wings, and with this Australian recipe that serves them with delicious grilled corn cobs, you are going to love them even more.

Serves: 10

Ingredients:
¼ cup honey
2 tablespoons soy sauce
Finely grated rind and juice of 1 lemon
1 tablespoon oil
1 teaspoon five spice
2 ½ pounds chicken wings
4 corn cobs, husks intact
¼ cup butter, at room temperature

Directions:
1. Mix the honey, soy sauce, lemon juice and rind, oil, and a teaspoon of five spice in a shallow platter. Put in the chicken wings and make sure to coat them well with the marinade. Place them into the refrigerator for at least one hour, or preferably overnight.
2. Prepare your barbecue by heating your grill to medium heat. Peel the corn husks, but don't remove them; only remove the silk. Each cob should be buttered and then rewrapped in its husk. You can tie it with a string.
3. Grill the corn on the barbecue for about 20 minutes, turning it often. If you see that corn is getting too brown, wrap each of the cobs in aluminum foil and move on with the grilling.
4. Grill the chicken wings for approximately 20 minutes, flipping regularly until they are completely cooked. Serve chicken and corn together.

Barbecued Lobster with Tomalley Butter

Lobster is a true specialty for eating and especially preparing, as you get to actually kill it during the preparation process

Serves: 2

Ingredients:
1-2 live lobster, about 1 ½ to 2 pounds each
5 ounces unsalted butter
1 red chili, sliced
2 lemons (1 juiced, 1 for garnish)
Very good-quality sea salt
Extra lemons, cut into cheeks

Directions:
1. Put the lobster in the freezer for about half an hour, or put it in a big dish filled with ice water. When it falls asleep, hit it between the eyes to kill it.
2. Prepare a big pot of boiling water and put in the lobster. Boil for approximately 5 minutes and move it to a big bowl with ice.
3. Split it in two and scoop the tomalley out. Use a skillet to melt the butter and then add the chili. Once the butter is melted, strain the tomalley into the butter by pressing it through a sieve. Put in a squeeze of lemon and mix it together.
4. Prepare the barbecue grill and set the heat to medium.
5. Use some of the butter to brush the lobster meat and grill for approximately 8 minutes, meat side directly on the grill. Besides the lobster, make sure to grill some lemon cheeks, placing them with flesh down.
6. Season with salt to your liking and serve with grilled lemon cheeks and remaining tomalley butter.

Grilled Lamb with Feta and Zucchini

If you need a quick solution for your family dinner, use this Australian lamb recipe to create an ideal summer meal everyone will love.

Serves: 4-6

Ingredients:
6 zucchinis, trimmed, and shaved into ribbons
Olive oil, to cook
12 lamb cutlets, French-trimmed
10 mint leaves, torn
3 ½ ounces feta, crumbled
2 tablespoons extra-virgin olive oil

Directions:
1. Coat the zucchinis with a bit of oil and season them to your liking with salt and pepper.
2. Prepare your barbecue by bringing it to a high level of heat. Grill the zucchinis for approximately 2 minutes on each side. Take them off the grill.
3. Season the lamb with salt and pepper and coat the cutlets with a tiny amount of oil. Grill over high heat for approximately two minutes per side or until it is medium-rare.
4. In a bowl, put the zucchinis, mint and feta. Sprinkle with oil and season it to your liking. Toss together to make a salad. Serve it with the cutlets.

Conclusion

Barbecue cooking will definitely brighten your life. It will enable you to prepare food just the way our ancestors did; it will also give you the option of enjoying it like in the old days – with your bare hands. After all, this is the way you should eat grilled food. Besides, barbecues are a great reason to get your family together or make a great party for your neighborhood or with friends you haven't seen for a long time. Food is prepared quickly on a grill and the chef can never be bored, as barbecues are actually one kind of theatre.

More Books from Sarah Spencer

Shown below are some of her other books. To check any of them out, just click on the book cover you like. Follow Sarah and join in her great love of cooking!

Thanksgiving
Feast Cookbook
The Very Best Classic and New Recipes
Sarah Spencer

CHRISTMAS
FEAST COOKBOOK
The Very Best Classic and New Recipes
SARAH SPENCER

DELICIOUS 200-CALORIE DESSERT RECIPES
Perfect for Your Sweet Tooth and Waistline!
SARAH SPENCER

SIMPLE PALEO SALAD
COOKBOOK
50 QUICK & EASY GLUTEN-FREE SALAD RECIPES
FEEL ENERGIZED, LOSE WEIGHT AND LOOK HEALTHY
SARAH SPENCER

Gluten Free
TODAY
36 QUICK & EASY LUNCH AND SNACK RECIPES
SARAH SPENCER

SPICE
IT UP!
THE BEST SPICE MIXING RECIPES FROM AROUND THE WORLD
SARAH SPENCER

Low Carb
Meals
Sarah Spencer

Smoothie
Bowls
50 Healing Smoothie Bowl Recipes
Sarah Spencer

Grateful Happiness
Living in the Present Moment
Letting Go of the Past
Sarah Spencer

5 Ingredient
Slow Cooker
Recipes
EASY 5 INGREDIENT CROCK POT COOKBOOK
Sarah Spencer

NO SUGAR ADDED
HEALTHY
FROZEN
DESSERT
Recipes
Ice Pop, Slush, Sorbet, Treat on Stick, Frozen Yogurt,
Frozen drink, Pie, Bar, Parfait and More
LOUISE DAVIDSON

Clean
Eating
Made Easy
WHOLESOME CLEAN EATING DIET RECIPES
Sarah Spencer

Appendix

Barbecue Grilling Times and Tips

BEEF	Size	Grilling Time	Internal Temperature in °F (Fahrenheit)
Steaks	3/4" thick	3 to 4 min/side 4 to 5 min/side	Medium rare 145 Medium 160
Kabobs	1 inch cubes	3 to 4 min/side	145 to 160
Hamburger patties	1/2" thick	3 min/side	160
Roast, rolled rump (indirect heat) Sirloin tip (indirect heat)	4 to 6 lbs. 3 1/2 to 4 lbs.	18 to 22 min/lb. 20 to 25 min/lb.	145 to 160
Ribs, Back	cut in 1 rib portions	10 min/side	160
Tenderloin	Half, 2 to 3 lbs. Whole, 4 to 6 lbs.	10 to 12 min/side 12 to 15 min/side	Medium rare 145 Medium 160

PORK	Size	Grilling Time	Internal Temperature in °F (Fahrenheit)
Chops, bone in or boneless	3/4" thick 1 1/2" thick	3 to 4 min/side 7 to 8 min/side	145
Tenderloin	1/2 to 1 1/2 lbs.	15 to 25 min. total	145
Ribs (indirect heat)	2 to 4 lbs.	1 1/2 to 2 hrs.	145
Patties, ground	1/2" thick	4 to 5 min/side	145
HAM	Size	Grilling Time	Internal Temperature in °F (Fahrenheit)
Fully cooked (indirect heat)	any size	8 to 10 min/lb.	140
Cook before eating (indirect heat)	Whole, 10 to 14 lbs. Half, 5 to 7 lbs. Portion, 3 to 4 lbs.	10 to 15 min/lb. 12 to 18 min/lb. 30 to 35 min/lb.	160

LAMB	Size	Grilling Time	Internal Temperature in °F (Fahrenheit)
Chops, shoulder, loin, or rib	1" thick	5 min/side	145 to 160
Steaks, sirloin, or leg	1" thick	5 min/side	145 to 160
Kabobs	1" cubes	4 min/side	145 to 160
Patties, ground	4 oz., 1/2" thick	3 min/side	160
Leg, butterflied	4 to 7 lbs.	40 to 50 min. total	145 to 160
VEAL	Size	Grilling Time	Internal Temperature in °F (Fahrenheit)
Chops, steaks	1" thick	5 to 7 min/side	145 to 160
Roast, boneless (indirect heat)	2 to 3 lbs.	18 to 20 min/lb.	145 to 160

CHICKEN	Size	Grilling Time	Internal Temperature in °F (Fahrenheit)
Whole (indirect heat), not stuffed	3 to 4 lbs. 5 to 7 lbs. 4 to 8 lbs.	60 to 75 min. 18 to 25 min./lb. 15 to 20 min/lb.	165 to 180 as measured in the thigh
Cornish hens	18 to 24 oz.	45 to 55 min.	
Breast halves, bone in boneless	6 to 8 oz. each 4 oz. each	10 to 15 min/side 7 to 8 min./side –	165 to 170
Other parts: Legs or thighs Drumsticks Wings,	4 to 8 oz. 4 oz. 2 to 3 oz.	10 to 15 min/side 8 to 12 min/side 8 to 12 min/side	165 to 180
TURKEY	Size	Grilling Time	Internal Temperature in °F (Fahrenheit)
Whole turkey (indirect heat)	8 to 12 lbs. 12 to 16 lbs. 16 to 24 lbs.	2 to 3 hrs. 3 to 4 hrs. 4 to 5 hrs.	165 to 180 as measured in the thigh
Breast, bone in boneless	4 to 7 lbs. 2 3/4 to 3 1/2 lbs.	1 to 1 3/4 hrs. 12 to 15 min/side	165 to 170
Thighs, drumsticks (indirect heat) Direct heat (precook 1 hr.)	8 to 16 oz.	1 1/2 to 2 hrs. 8 to 10 min/side	165 to 180

Tips for successful and safe barbecuing:

- To make sure that harmful bacteria, sometime present in uncooked meat and poultry, are destroyed during the cooking process, you must make sure that the internal temperature is high enough for safe consumption. Always use a meat thermometer inserted in the thickest part without touching any bones. Research from the U.S. Department of Agriculture (USDA) states that the color of the meat is not a dependable indicator meat or poultry has reached a temperature high enough to destroy harmful bacteria that may be present.
- Follow this chart for approximate cooking times, Outdoor grills can vary in heat.
- Use barbecue sauce during the last 15 to 30 minutes of grilling to prevent excess browning or burning resulting from the sugars of the sauce.
- USDA recommends cooking pork, beef, veal, lamb chops, ribs and steaks until it reaches a minimum internal temperature of 145°F and then let rest at least 3 minutes before slicing or consuming.
- Although it is safe to eat poultry with an internal temperature of 165°F, the flavors and the texture are best when the internal temperature reaches 170°F to 180°F

Source: Food Safety and Inspection Service, USDA

Cooking Conversion Charts

Volumes

US Fluid Oz.	US	US Dry Oz.	Metric Liquid ml
¼ oz.	2 tsp.	1 oz.	10 ml.
½ oz.	1 tbsp.	2 oz.	15 ml.
1 oz.	2 tbsp.	3 oz.	30 ml.
2 oz.	¼ cup	3½ oz.	60 ml.
4 oz.	½ cup	4 oz.	125 ml.
6 oz.	¾ cup	6 oz.	175 ml.
8 oz.	1 cup	8 oz.	250 ml.

Tsp.= teaspoon - tbsp.= tablespoon – oz.= ounce – ml.= millimeter

Oven Temperatures

Celsius (°C)	Fahrenheit (°F)
90	220
110	225
120	250
140	275
150	300
160	325
180	350
190	375
200	400
215	425
230	450
250	475
260	500

Printed in Great Britain
by Amazon